GW01418605

How Can We Be Free?

How Can We
Be Free?

Christine Dodd

DARTON, LONGMAN AND TODD
LONDON

First published in 1992 by
Darton, Longman and Todd Ltd
89 Lillie Road, London SW6 1UD

© 1992 Christine Dodd

ISBN 0–232–51925–0

A catalogue record for this book is available
from the British Library

The Scripture quotations are taken from the
New Jerusalem Bible, published and copyright 1985 by
Darton, Longman and Todd Ltd and Doubleday & Co Inc
and used by permission of the publishers

Cover: *Le Bec du Hoc, Grandcamp* (1885) by Georges Seurat
The Tate Gallery, London

Phototypeset in 10/12 pt Trump by Intype, London
Printed and bound in Great Britain
at the University Press, Cambridge

Contents

◆━━━◆

Introduction

◆━━━◆

THE WRITINGS OF THE BIBLE – the Scriptures – are the Word of God. They are of supreme importance to all Christians and to all who wish to know and understand the meaning of Christianity. The Bible should be in every Christian home. Every aspect of Christian life and worship should reflect in some way what God says to his people. Catholics have not always been very good at reading and studying the Bible. In 1965 during the Second Vatican Council a document on Scripture as the Word of God (*Dei Verbum*) was published. This has had a marked effect in laying the foundations for an official programme of encouragement to Catholics to make the Bible central to their lives.

Much has happened since then. Every public act of worship has its reading from Scripture. Scripture (both Old and New Testaments) has a significant place in all religious education programmes, whether for adults or for children. The lectionary for the readings at daily and Sunday Mass covers a large amount of Scripture during its three-year cycle. Familiar acts of devotion like the Rosary and the Stations of the Cross have become far more scripturally based.

The positive value of this is obvious enough. But it has also meant that many Catholics have been thrown in at the deep end. They are a little like the Ethiopian in his carriage on the way home from Jerusalem who was reading some Scripture. Philip the Deacon heard him and asked him if he understood what he was reading. 'How can I,' the man said, 'unless I have someone to guide me?' (Acts 8:26–40). Most of us do need help if we are to understand what we are reading. It is not that the language of Scripture is particularly difficult; it is rather that its context is so often unfamiliar.

I warmly welcome this series of *Scripture for Living.* Its particular value is that it helps us to see how Scripture is relevant to our daily lives. There are many other books for scholars. This series is for ordinary Christians who treasure Scripture, know for certain that it is of fundamental importance, but who are not sure how to make sense of what they read or how to relate it to their daily lives and experiences.

The pattern of the series is a story, bible passage, commentary, reflection and prayer. There is a natural progression in this. The writings in the Bible (which form a whole library really) are about people trying to recognise God in their lives. So the context is just everyday life – the stuff of story. Story leads on naturally to Scripture because Scripture is itself about life in all its variety. So it speaks of love and hate, success and failure, death and resurrection; almost every imaginable human failing and strength finds place in it, simply because it is about real people. The commentary is an aid to understanding. Then, since the ultimate purpose of Scripture is to lead people closer to God, the text finishes with a prayer which ties together what has gone before and shows how our daily lives can be enriched.

The series is ideal for use in groups as well as by individuals. I wish it every success.

+ DAVID KONSTANT
Bishop of Leeds

Preface

FREEDOM IS A SLIPPERY WORD. To one person it may mean the removal, by some outside power, of whatever holds them captive; the release of a prisoner from bondage. To others freedom has an inner quality. It is the peace of mind which exists despite a painful situation that will never go away such as grief or pain. For them to discover freedom is to discover an inner liberation despite outside circumstances. However we may think of it freedom has something to do with liberation, space to be oneself, and release from oppression.

All sorts of things enslave us. We are held captive by a whole range of pressures, attitudes and circumstances. Who can set us free from the expectations other people have of us or the expectations we have of ourselves? Who can liberate us from the oppression of injustice or the pain of guilt? We want to be released from our own passions and desires and temperaments. We want to be free to be ourselves and to help others to be free from whatever oppresses them.

This longing for freedom is deep within us but our experiences of life often tell us that it is an unattainable dream. No matter how hard we try there will always be those situations where we are captive to the pain and grief that is part of being human and nothing can remove it from us.

This book is not about the unattainable. It is about

how we can be set free within the situations in which
we find ourselves. To use the words of St Paul, it is about
living in 'the glorious liberty of the children of God'.
Down the generations countless men and women have
discovered the God who can set them free.

The Bible is about that liberating action of God. It is
as we reflect on their experiences of his work within and
around them that we can discover that the same love
which set them free offers liberty to us as well. Their
stories and ours are not so different. What God offers to
them he offers to us.

CHRISTINE DODD

Freedom from Expectations

◄━━━━━►

HELEN WAS THE ELDEST of three children and there was no doubt about it, she was very bright. Like many others she experienced the conscious and unconscious pressure of always being the oldest child. The expectations that her parents had of her were that she would be an example for the younger children and so she felt that she must do well at everything.

As an adult, Helen knew that she carried within her the burden of those expectations and she found it very difficult to be free of them. Although her younger brother and sister were now grown up too, somehow the effect of always having high expectations heaped upon her had left their mark. Now married and with a small child of her own, she was determined that when the next baby came along she would not cause her oldest child any such problems.

Chris was the youngest member of Helen's family. The expectations on him were that he would always live up to the example of his sister. He too was bright, but simply because she was older he was always having to catch up with her, something he never managed to achieve. Consequently he always felt that his parents were disappointed in him. When he did fail to achieve the same standard as Helen academically, it became an unspoken assumption in the family that Chris would never go far. Expectations plummeted and Chris's sense of self-worth plummeted with it. He sensed that his parents now had very low expectations of him and were content to let him muddle along. The result was that that was exactly what he did. He gave up trying. He ceased to believe in his capabilities. He lived down to their expectations just as Helen lived up to them.

It was on the night that the results of his GCSEs had come through that Chris overheard Helen's conversation with his parents. 'You never pushed him like you pushed me so why are you surprised?' asked Helen. 'That's not fair,' replied her mother, 'Chris has had just the same opportunities as you.' 'Yes, but your expectations of him are never the same. You never really expected him to do well.' 'Well lets face it,' said her mother, 'he is not as bright as you.' Chris didn't wait to hear the rest of the conversation. All his worst fears had been confirmed. The expectation his mother had of him was that he would never make good. Well, he would show them.

◀▬▬▶

Here is St Mark's account of Jesus coming to his home town and what happened when he came face to face with the expectations his own people had of him.

Leaving that district, he [Jesus] went to his home town, and his disciples accompanied him. With the coming of the Sabbath he began teaching in the synagogue, and most of them were astonished when they heard him. They said, 'Where did the man get all this? What is this wisdom that has been granted him, and these miracles that are worked through him? This is the carpenter, surely, the son of Mary, the brother of James and Joseph and Jude and Simon? His sisters, too, are they not here with us?' and they would not accept him. And Jesus said to them, 'A prophet is despised only in his own country, among his own relations and in his own house'; and he could work no miracle there, except that he cured a few sick people by laying his hands on them. He was amazed at their lack of faith.

(Mark 6:1–6)

◆━━━◆

Several things are said in this story about expectations. It is an important passage in Mark because the early Church had somehow to work out why the gospel was rejected by Jesus' own people when others were accepting it and it was spreading rapidly among the Gentiles. The answer to this difficulty lay in the assertion that Jesus' rejection was all part of God's plan and that part of that plan was the freedom to accept or reject him.

For those around Jesus the common expectation was that the Messiah would be a glorious figure who would champion the cause of his people through strength and power. Jesus' exercise of his status was quite contrary to this expectation. This Messiah was to 'conquer' not through power or force, but through humiliation, suffering and death and the kingdom he came to build is not to be established through might of arms but through living a life of justice and truth. Small wonder, then, that people misunderstood and rejected him. If we look carefully at the story we notice how the people's expectations of Jesus are different and are hampering their acceptance of him which would lead them to freedom. To begin with, the people simply fail to see, they look only at what they know. They had probably grown up with this family and they found it incredibly difficult to expect Jesus to be anything other than what he had always been, the local village tradesman. Blindness and failure to look and see limit their understanding and provoke their reaction and rejection. Jesus doesn't fit in with their expectations.

Jesus' failure to live down to the people's expectations of him has another effect on them. They seem to realise that something extraordinary is happening here. We read that they are impressed by his teaching. They have heard of his healing powers. This very awareness seems to irritate them. It is almost as if they hold a grudge against Jesus who shares the same humble origins but has broken out of the expectations they have of him. 'This is the carpenter, surely, the son of Mary.' They seem to think that Jesus has no right to have what they have not, to be what they are not. Sometimes envy and jealousy cause us to put limits on what we expect of others and what they expect of us.

Another limiting factor on the people's ability to see who Jesus really is, is their expectation about how God works. They simply cannot accept that God will work in this way through someone they know. If Jesus had such humble origins and they knew that he had, how could he come from God? They cling to the idea of what they expect the Messiah to be and Jesus does not fit into this expectation. The people cannot deny his ability or his work and it raises all the right questions for them ('Where did the man get all this?') but their expectation prevents them giving a response that would lead them into new understanding.

When we turn to Jesus we see that his reaction to the expectation that the people have of him is twofold. First, he refuses to be moulded by it. They had him fitted into a neat box but he refused to be shut in it. As such his actions and words challenged them to decide for or against him; to take offence or to follow. Second, Jesus could 'work no miracle there'. He was amazed at their lack of faith. The expectations they had effectively prevented him working there. It is elsewhere away from his home town that people believe and he is able to proclaim the kingdom. These people have different expectations and perhaps no expectations of him at all. It is because they are open to hear and to see and are not limited by what they *think* they should be hearing and seeing that they can respond and be led into new understanding and freedom.

There are a number of ways this story can help us to be free of the power that the expectations of others have over us.

Seeing. We need to recognise that sometimes people's expectations are limited or moulded simply by what they see. This is especially true of people who are close to us, just as it was true of the people who knew Jesus well. They do not expect us to be anything other than what they have always known us to be. So if we go outside those boundaries questions are certain to be raised. Recognising that this is what can happen can liberate us. If we are prepared for people to be surprised then we are not as likely to be imprisoned and unable to move.

Threatening. Next, the people in the story see something they were not expecting. They cannot deny that someone different and special is among them and yet this is in conflict with what they have always thought Jesus to be. His words and deeds irritate them because he breaks out of their low expectations of him. Similarly, if we exceed the expectations people have of us we are likely to upset the applecart. People are confused, irritated, or plain envious that we do not fit in with the preconceived pattern they had for us. It provokes a need to reassess us, something others may prefer not to do, for it means that they have to admit their experience of us was wrong. So, it should not surprise us if people feel threatened or challenged when we do not fit into the neat box they have made for us. It may even happen that people will reject us because of the way we fail to fit into their expectations. Jesus experienced this too, but he also came across people open enough to see who he really was. And there are people around us who are open enough to see who we really are and all the potential that we have. This, too, can liberate us.

Refusal to be moulded. Jesus himself gives us the clue to the way to discover freedom from false expectations, whether those expectations are too high or too low. His refusal to be moulded is the first. God created us to be unique individuals with our own unique personalities, gifts and talents. To live in freedom means to be what God intended us to be and to have the sort of expectation of ourselves that he has of us. His expectation is that we should be ourselves, our true selves. Where others have expectations which prevent us from being this, then we should be refused to be moulded by them. That does not give us a free hand to do as we like. It does give us permission to refuse to be held down by what others think we can or should be and not to be pushed into something for which we are not equipped because others expect it of us. The passage and Jesus' reaction give us permission to be ourselves.

The second clue to gaining freedom from false expectations is Jesus' understanding that he will be misunderstood and that it is only away from his home that he will gain a positive response. Often people whose expectations of us are either different from those at home, or who do not really have any expectation of us at all, can help us. They enable us to keep a balance and to see that we need not be bound by expectations which are too high or by expectations which are too low. Realising that different people expect different things from us releases us to be ourselves.

One final point needs to be made. Sometimes we are enslaved by the expectations we have of ourselves. We expect either too much or not enough of ourselves. It is how we can walk towards freedom from these expectations that we shall turn to in the next chapter.

FOR REFLECTION

1. Take a pen and piece of paper.
2. Consciously place yourself in the presence of God.
3. List down on the paper the major areas and people in your life e.g. your family, work, hobbies etc. Do this on the left-hand side of the paper. On the right-hand side of the paper list what you think are the expectations others have of you in each of these areas.
4. Which expectations do you find: invalid? too high? too low?
5. What could you do about all this?

PRAYER

In your own words place what you have discovered in the presence of God. You may like to use this psalm as an act of trust.

> Yahweh is my light and my salvation,
>   whom should I fear?
> Yahweh is the fortress of my life,
>   whom should I dread?
>
> Though an army pitch camp against me,
>   my heart will not fear,
> though war break out against me,
>   my trust will never be shaken.
>
> This I believe: I shall see the goodness of Yahweh,
>   in the land of the living.
> Put your hope in Yahweh, be strong, let your heart
>   be bold,
>   put your hope in Yahweh.
>
>   (Psalm 27:1, 3,13–14)

Freedom from Myself

ON THE SURFACE Colin seemed to be a very cheerful and contented person. He was a good mixer and able to make friends easily. He was the sort of person who seemed interested in countless activities and was always surprising people by taking up unexpected and new hobbies. Those who knew Colin well also knew that there was a very different side to him. Colin himself knew only too well that the person others saw was not the real Colin.

When Colin was honest with himself, and he would never have said this to other people, he would admit to being a mass of conflicting desires, aspirations and disappointments. A good deal of what others saw was just a front to prevent them from getting close to him and to cover up his own insecurity about himself. On the one hand Colin had very low expectations of himself. He never thought he was as good as other people. He never thought he could achieve anything so he would rush from one activity to another, beginning with great enthusiasm but leaving when things began to get difficult. On the other hand he had very high expectations of himself. He wanted to be able to overcome those areas of himself where he felt at fault. But he could never manage it. All that he longed to be and do and say was one thing, the achieving of it was quite another. These high expectations made him think even less of himself. In fact,

Colin's sense of self-worth was extremely low. So Colin would torture himself, on the one hand thinking he could do nothing, and on the other having such high and unachievable expectations of himself.

In the face of what he knew himself to be, Colin wondered if it was ever possible to achieve freedom from himself. It seemed to him that nothing and no one could really help him. His friends clearly liked him. Often they would compliment him and affirm him, but even so Colin was less than happy with the person he knew himself to be. If the truth were known, he felt himself to be a hopeless case and that it was beyond the power of anyone to set him free from himself.

◆━━━◆

The story of the meeting between the 'demoniac legion' and Jesus allows us to reflect on the power of Christ to overcome the 'demons' of self-doubt and false expectations that we have of ourselves. The story is told to us by Matthew, Mark and Luke. Here is Mark's account.

They reached the territory of the Gerasenes on the other side of the lake, and when he [Jesus] disembarked, a man with an unclean spirit at once came out from the tombs towards him. The man lived in the tombs and no one could secure him any more, even with a chain, because he had often been secured with fetters and chains but had snapped the chains and broken the fetters, and no one had the strength to control him. All night and all day, among the tombs and in the mountains, he would howl and gash himself with stones. Catching sight of Jesus from a distance, he ran up and fell at his feet and shouted at the top of his voice, 'What do you want with me, Jesus, Son of the Most High God? In God's name do not torture me!' For Jesus had been saying to him, 'Come out of the man, unclean spirit.' Then he asked 'What is your name?' He answered, 'My

*name is Legion, for there are many of us.' And he begged
him earnestly not to send them out of the district. Now
on the mountainside there was a great herd of pigs feed-
ing, and the unclean spirits begged him, 'Send us into
the pigs, let us go into them.' So he gave them leave.
With that the unclean spirits came out and went into
the herd of pigs, and the herd of about two thousand
pigs charged down the cliff into the lake and there they
were drowned. The men looking after them ran off and
told their story in the city and in the country round-
about; and the people came to see what had really happened. They came to Jesus and saw the demoniac sitting
there – the man who had had the legion in him – properly
dressed and in his full senses, and they were afraid. And
those who had witnessed it reported what had happened
to the demoniac and what had become of the pigs. Then
they began to implore Jesus to leave their neighbour-
hood. As he was getting into the boat, the man who had
been possessed begged to be allowed to stay with him.
Jesus would not let him but said to him, 'Go home to
your people and tell them all that the Lord in his mercy
has done for you.' So the man went off and proceeded
to proclaim in the Decapolis all that Jesus had done for
him. And everyone was amazed.*

(Mark 5:1–20)

━━◆━━

This story occurs in Mark after the story of Jesus calming
the storm at sea, a story which showed his power over
nature and the chaos of the deep. The curing of the
demoniac shows his power over the inner chaos of an
individual personified by the demons. Let us look at the
different parts of the story.

We see first of all that the man lives in the tombs, these
were commonly believed to be the haunt of demons. His
condition is given to us in some detail so that we can
see what a hopeless state he is in and appreciate Jesus'

power to do something about it and free him from it. No one else in the area had been able to do anything with this man; he was beyond human help, made a prisoner by his affliction and by the inability of the community to cope with it.

The story progresses as we read of the man's reaction to the sight of Jesus. Recognising who he is, he falls at Jesus' feet, an attitude of submission and worship, and he calls him 'Jesus, Son of the Most High God'. Next comes a haunting phrase, 'In God's name do not torture me!'. We have to remember that to gain power over another it was vital to know their name. It is as if the demon tried to gain power over Jesus by using his name and title (Jesus, Son of the Most High God). Realising this cannot happen he begs Jesus not to punish him but to give him leave to go elsewhere. Jesus in his turn, asks the name of the demon and receives an immediate response showing that he does have power over this destructive force that the man experiences.

The story ends with the account of the demons entering the pigs and the reaction of the crowd. This is used by Mark to show how complete this miracle was. It was a commonly held belief that when a demon was exorcised it would take itself off in a rage and cause havoc elsewhere, so the rushing of the pigs down the cliff, coupled with the change in the man, would be seen by the onlooker as the proof of the miracle that Jesus had done. This power of Jesus is so complete that the crowd cannot cope with it and they beg him to leave their land.

It is easy when reading a passage like this to get over concerned with the question of demons and possession. What we should remember, however, is the crunch point of the story. The man is in a hopeless situation but Jesus has the power to free him from all that enslaves him. It is this message that is important for us as we try to gain freedom from our own 'demons'.

Powerlessness. An awareness that we are enslaved is common to most of us. We may feel at the mercy of a variety of 'demons' within ourselves. It may be our anger, or our lack of self-worth, or our inability to believe that others can see anything good in us. We may believe ourselves to be unloved and unlovable, the victims of any one of a number of different forces. These forces imprison us and prevent us from being the person we might be. They prevent us from living in freedom. As if that was not enough, we also find ourselves completely powerless to do anything about them. Like the man in the tombs we are in a hopeless condition and we so often 'gash' ourselves 'with stones' and 'howl' at our impotence to conquer the 'demons' within us.

The inability we know we have to help ourselves can be increased by discovering that others may not be able to release us either. Like the crowd in the story, they are powerless in our battle to live a truly free life. They may be able to affirm us and encourage us; they can assure us that we are loved and respected for what we are but the demons can still remain, lurking in our depths and ready to surface when we least expect them.

The coming of Jesus into our powerlessness. It is into this situation that Jesus comes, knowing all the pain and misery we cause ourselves and the self-doubt we experience. In the story we saw that the first reaction of the man was to cry out at the approach of Jesus 'do not torture me'. Liberation from myself means allowing myself to be open to the approach of Jesus. But his approach can fill us with dread because misguidedly we fear that if we allow him access he may confirm all our worst fears about ourselves. We are afraid that he will condemn and punish us for not being what we could be; that he will do to us what he did to the demons. We may also fear that his action in coming to us may take from us what little we have and that, in driving out the demons, we may be left with nothing but a terrible void.

These fears are, of course, groundless. We have no cause to be afraid. The casting out of the 'demons' will free us to be what we have the potential to be. To free us from the burden a lack of self-worth can impose upon us. In casting out the 'demons' Jesus does not destroy us. He sets us free.

The new life of freedom with Christ. The people who came to see what had happened discovered the demoniac sitting there with Jesus and they were amazed. One of the reasons we fear to be open both with God and with others is what they will think of us. We are afraid that if they see 'the real me' it will be so unlike the image presented on the surface that they will be as amazed as the crowd was at seeing the healed demoniac. We fear that if we let them see the true self they will care less about us; that they will discover that we are even more unlovable than we already believe ourselves to be. The truth is that being open with God and with people we trust and allowing them to act in our lives will lead us to the freedom of sitting in the presence of Jesus, just as the demoniac did. We and those around us would be amazed at how God can transform us given the opportunity.

The new life of freedom with others. Finally the healed man longs to go with Jesus but is commanded to stay with his own people and 'tell them all that the Lord in his mercy has done for you.' Never before had he had the freedom to relate to others like this. His affliction had excluded him from human companionship and community. Jesus' power in enabling him to be his true self gave him new scope and new freedom he had never experienced before. He could be his real self with others. Our enslavement to our own images of ourselves and our inability to be free to be what God wants us to be curtails our relationships and contacts with others. In giving us the freedom to be ourselves Jesus releases us to a new life with others. The need to hide, to cope with our lack

of self-worth and our continual torturing of ourselves
with impossible aims and expectations is removed. All
that potential to grow into a full human being is released
and with it the responsibility to enable others to discover
that same freedom.

FOR REFLECTION

1. Place yourself in the presence of God.
2. Ask yourself: What do you like most about yourself?
    What do you dislike most about yourself? In what
    way does your image of yourself enslave you? What
    'demons' prevent you from being your true self?
3. Imagine yourself amongst the crowd of onlookers
    when Jesus meets the demoniac. Seeing what Jesus
    does fills them with fear and they implore him to go
    away. Jesus turns to you. He sees the 'demon' in you.
    He offers to release you. How do you respond?

PRAYER

Close with a prayer of your own or make these words of
St Paul your own.

> And really, I know of nothing good living in me – in
> my natural self, that is – for though the will to do what
> is good is in me, the power to do it is not: the good
> thing I want to do, I never do; the evil thing which I
> do not want – that is what I do. But every time I do
> what I do not want to do, then it is not myself acting
> but the sin that lives in me.
>
> So I find this rule: that for me, where I want to do
> nothing but good, evil is close at my side. In my inmost
> self I dearly love God's law, but I see that acting on
> my body there is a different law which battles against
> the law in my mind. So I am brought to be a prisoner
> of that law of sin which lives inside my body.

What a wretched man I am! Who will rescue me from this body doomed to death? God – thanks be to him – through Jesus Christ our Lord.

(Romans 7:18–25)

Freedom from the Past

◆━━◆

Walking into Dorothy's sitting room was like stepping back in time. The furniture, the china in the china cabinet and the pictures all reminded the visitor of the 1930s. On the sideboard were the photographs of her only daughter, Elaine, on her wedding day and there were several of the grandchildren. Standing in pride of place on the mantelpiece was the photograph of Dorothy's husband. It showed a handsome young soldier in uniform. His smile still radiated from a now fading picture.

Bill and Dorothy had married in 1940. It was eighteen months later that Bill had been killed and for most of those eighteen months the couple had been separated. Bill had never seen Elaine. She was born four months after his death. Dorothy had never really recovered from what had happened. She had survived and brought up her daughter with love and care but never really let go of the past. She adored her grandchildren but her life was still dominated by those few short months with Bill and thoughts of all the years they might have had were still uppermost in her mind. The past so dominated her life that ever since Bill's death Dorothy had felt she was existing rather than living.

Elaine found her mother's inability to let go of the past difficult to handle. She had been raised on stories about the father she had never seen and she had grown up believing him to be nearly perfect. As she got older she found it increasingly difficult to cope with the way her mother lived in the past. Bringing friends home once or twice was not too bad because her mother usually refrained from talking about her father. But if friends came round frequently, sooner or later they would be subjected to a long tale about the war and what it had done to her family.

Veronica had known Dorothy for a long time. They had shared the same office many years ago. She had become used to hearing the same stories over and over again but she couldn't help thinking that Dorothy had almost ceased to live when Bill had died. Each time Veronica called at the house she knew that Dorothy would eventually bring the conversation around to something that happened in those eighteen months of her life with Bill. Veronica knew that this was not deliberate but Dorothy's way of trying to cope. She knew it was more to do with Dorothy's inability to let go of the past than anything else.

Veronica also noticed that Dorothy's attitude to almost any European was distant and sometimes hostile. Once, she had managed to persuade Dorothy to go on holiday and together they had travelled to Switzerland. It was a disaster. It was almost as if Dorothy blamed anyone from the other side of the English Channel for Bill's death even if they and their nation had been blameless. This bitterness had grown rather than diminished over the years. Dorothy seemed unable to contemplate acceptance of what had happened, let alone any thought of forgiveness for those who had caused it. Because the grandchildren were grown up and no longer the frequent visitors they used to be, Veronica feared that Dorothy would become more and more immersed in the past; trying to live a life that had been lost and more and more unable to face the future.

Like Dorothy, most of us look back at the past with a mixture of joy and sorrow. Like her, we can never ignore the past for, to a large extent, we are what the past has made us. Our lives have been shaped by what has happened to us, the people we have met, the conversations we have had, the experiences we have been through. In one sense then, we must be able to look back to the past and to learn from it. But the past can also be a heavy chain. There are times when memories can so dominate us that our lives are centred, not in the present, but in the years that have gone before. This domination can be a real enslavement. It prevents us from living life to the full. It is at these times that we need to find the freedom that God offers. We need to find a way of coping with the past, of accepting it and of looking forward to the future.

***

In the Book of Genesis Abraham (or Abram as he was known at the time) is called to let go of the past in return for a new life. Here is the story of Abraham's call and God's promise.

Yahweh said to Abram, 'Leave your country, your kindred and your father's house for a country which I shall show you; and I shall make you a great nation, I shall bless you and make your name famous; you are to be a blessing.

> *I shall bless those who bless you,*
> *and shall curse those who curse you,*
> *and all clans on earth,*
> *will bless themselves by you.*

So Abram went as Yahweh told him, and Lot went with him. Abram was seventy-five years old when he left Haran. Abram took his wife Sarai, his nephew Lot, all the possessions they had amassed and the people they had acquired in Haran. They set off for the land of Canaan and arrived there.

Abram passed through the land as far as the holy place at Shechem, the Oak of Moreh. The Canaanites were in the country at the time. Yahweh appeared to Abram and said, 'I shall give this country to your progeny.' And there, Abram built an altar to Yahweh who had appeared to him. From there he moved on to the mountainous district east of Bethel, where he pitched his tent, with Bethel to the west and Ai to the east. There he built an altar to Yahweh and invoked the name of Yahweh. Then Abram made his way stage by stage to the Negeb.

(Genesis 12:1–9)

This passage is one of the great 'journey' stories in the Bible. It tells of God's call to Abraham to leave the past in Haran and set out towards a new future. Abraham is called to leave his country, his family, and his father's house to step out towards a new land. In other words he is called to let go of the past.

The Abraham stories in Genesis are largely about the promises God makes and the way these promises are to become reality. Here God promises that in letting go Abraham will be rewarded handsomely. He and his descendants will become 'a great nation'. He will be blessed. Later we read that this will happen through Isaac, Abraham and Sarai's son. Through Isaac the great promises of God will come true. Later, when God called Abraham to take Isaac up the mountain and offer him as a sacrifice he asked Abraham to sacrifice the whole future; the future that through Isaac God would build up a great nation. Not only is there the call to give up the past but to give up the future as well. But that part of Abraham's life is still to come and is another story. What is important in this passage is that Abraham is willing to leave the place he knows and to take up a nomadic lifestyle journeying towards the land God will show him.

We can notice four things about this passage which

can help us deal with our own past. First, the call of God is to let go of the past *completely*. Notice that there are stages of letting go. Abraham is initially called to leave first 'your country'. Then the call is narrowed down to leave 'your kindred' and finally to leave 'your father's house'. The giving up of each of these is difficult. Leaving your country is hard but not as difficult as leaving your family. Leaving your family is hard but not like leaving the father's house with all its past associations and the knowledge that you are leaving the place and the people that have made you what you are. Leaving each of these calls for faith and trust that the past is in God's hands and so is the future.

Secondly, Abraham was not a young man. According to the Bible he was 75 years old when he left Haran. Letting go and setting out for a new beginning could not have been easy after so long a time. Such a move takes great courage.

Thirdly the rest of the passage tells us that Abraham travelled extensively. He moves on from one place to another. He has no settled home. It is one long journey.

Finally we are told that on his travels Abraham builds an altar to the Lord. This happens twice on the journey, once at the Oak of Moreh and once in the mountains east of Bethel. His journey was thus made in the presence of God, and he acknowledges that God is leading him.

The Abraham journey away from the past recorded for us in Genesis 12 can give us clues as to how God can help us find our own freedom from memories which may hold us in their grip. The four things we noticed about Abraham's attitude can apply to us as well.

We notice that the call to let go was difficult. First Abraham was called to give up his country, then his family, then his father's house. No letting go of the past is easy. It takes time, and for us too it may happen by degrees. What is essential is that somehow we do learn to let the past go into the hands of God. Perhaps this letting go will be a bit at a time, our equivalent of the letting go of the country, the family, the father's house. Perhaps we shall have to let go of the same things many times, because often we shall find ourselves still haunted by the same memories. We need to be patient with ourselves. Healing from past hurts and experiences will not happen suddenly.

Next we saw that Abraham was an old man. After so long a time letting go could not have been easy. But his age did not prevent Abraham finding his new beginning. However difficult letting go may seem and however deep-seated our attachment to the past may appear, the call to set out for the new country applies to us. Like Abraham it will take courage to move our sights from the past to the present and the future but freedom comes to those who have the courage to look forwards, not backwards.

Thirdly, we saw that Abraham was always on the move. He pitched camp but then he moved on making his journey 'stage by stage' to the Negeb. The journey from enslavement to the past into the new land which God wishes to give us will be made 'stage by stage'. We are making a journey towards freedom. We should be always on the move, travelling towards that fullness of life that Christ promised. We find our freedom, not in standing still, looking mournfully over our shoulders but in offering the past to God and moving towards him who loves us no matter what the past has been.

Finally we saw that Abraham twice built an altar to God on his journey. It was not as if God called him to give up the past, sent him off on his journey, and then left him to get on with coping with the future. He appears to Abraham on the journey and Abraham responds. In his case, it is by building an altar. So too, God calls us to freedom from the past. He does not leave us alone on the road towards that freedom. He assures us of his presence. The past will always be with us. We cannot escape it.

No doubt Abraham would always have memories of Haran. Yet the past need not dominate us. It need not enslave us. Like Abraham we are called by God to let go knowing that he will accompany us on our journey to the freedom he offers. That journey will be one he will make with us, calling us like Abraham to respond.

FOR REFLECTION

1. Place yourself in the presence of God and ask him to help you honestly face yourself and all that has happened to you in the past.
2. Read Abraham's story again.
3. Imagine yourself as Abraham. What would you most regret leaving behind? Would it be people or a sense of security or identity, or something else?
4. Listen to God calling you to let go of your past. What is the most difficult memory to release into the hands of God? Is there anything in the past of which you are afraid to let go? Why?
5. Try to give the past to God, knowing that he has power to release you from its hurts and ties. You may like to do this by imagining yourself at the foot of the Cross. Place each part of the past that you wish to give to God at the feet of Jesus. Take your time over this. When you have finished *leave the past there*. You may like to imagine yourself leaving the Cross and facing the living Christ with his promise of freedom.

PRAYER

Close with a prayer in your own words. If you find this difficult you may like to use the following:

Lord you have been our refuge
from age to age.

Before the mountains were born,
before the earth and the world came to birth,
from eternity to eternity you are God.

Teach us to count up the days that are ours,
and we shall come to the heart of wisdom.
Come back, Yahweh! How long must we wait?
Take pity on your servants.

Each morning fill us with your faithful love,
we shall sing and be happy all our days;
let our joy be as long as the time that you afflicted us,
the years when we experienced disaster.

Show your servants the deeds you do,
Let their children enjoy your splendour!
May the sweetness of the Lord be upon us,
To confirm the work we have done!

(Psalm 90:1–2, 12–17)

Freedom from the Fear of the Future

◆━━━━◆

Margaret LIVED HER LIFE in a state of constant fear of what might happen. Malcolm, her husband, had suffered his heart attack seven years ago. Two years later he had another. It was touch and go. He had recovered well but Margaret lived with the fear that it would happen again and this time Malcolm would not survive.

Margaret's fears of the future were natural but she found that fears about 'what might happen' were beginning to dominate her life with Malcolm. He would go out to potter in the garden and Margaret would spend the time by the window just in case he collapsed. She would panic every time he was ten minutes late home from work and worse still, she spent hours imagining what the future *might* hold. She would sit in the evenings with a whole string of 'what ifs' going through her mind. What if he had a stroke? What if he was in hospital for weeks? Above all, what if he died? Life would seem so empty, so pointless without him. How would she cope?

Malcolm was aware of some, if not all, of these fears. He would gently try to tell her that they had today to live for and what was the point of spoiling it by forever thinking about something which might, or might not, happen tomorrow. Margaret knew that he was right but she loved him, and for all her efforts to live for today, the fear of losing him dominated her. She tried not to let it show but it permeated everything she did and almost everything she thought.

At some time or other most of us fear the future. This is natural for us, especially if it is connected, like Margaret, with someone we love. There would be something dreadfully wrong if we did not fear losing someone who is close to us. But fear of the future can take many forms. The fear may be of something known to us, something we know will happen. More often the fear is connected with the unknown; fears of what *might* be. We can usually manage to cope if we know what the future holds even though it may seem black. It is when we do not know what it will bring and our future is full of the imagined horrors of things that might happen that our fears are worse and it is then that they have such power over us. This fear of the unknown future may be concentrated on practical matters. How will we manage, what will happen to us? Or our fears may be concentrated on more personal dilemmas – will we have the strength to cope? How will we react as a person? Sometimes we fear that what happens in the future may damage our faith. Such fears do exist and we cannot get away from them. We have to learn how to live with our worries about tomorrow. Being fearful of the future is one thing, but being so enslaved by it that we are unable to function properly because of it is quite another. Like Margaret, we can end up failing to enjoy today because of our worries about tomorrow. Is there any way of being released from this fear of the future which can hold us in its grip?

◆━━━━━◆

The account in St John's Gospel of the disciples' experience of the risen Christ suggests a way of coping with our fears of the future.

In the evening of that same day, the first day of the

*week, the doors were closed in the room where the dis-
ciples were, for fear of the Jews. Jesus came and stood
among them. He said to them, 'Peace be with you,' and,
after saying this, he showed them his hands and his side.
The disciples were filled with joy at seeing the Lord and
he said to them again, 'Peace be with you.'*

*Thomas, called the Twin, who was one of the twelve,
was not with them when Jesus came. So the other disciples said to him, 'We have seen the Lord,' but he
answered, 'Unless I can see the holes that the nails made
in his hands and can put my finger into the holes they
made, and unless I can put my hand into his side, I
refuse to believe.' Eight days later the disciples were in
the house again and Thomas was with them. The doors
were closed but Jesus came in and stood among them.
'Peace be with you,' he said. Then he spoke to Thomas,
'Put your finger here; look, here are my hands. Give me
your hand; put it into my side. Do not be unbelieving
any more but believe.' Thomas replied, 'My Lord and
my God!' Jesus said to him:*

> *You believe because you can see me.*
> *Blessed are those who have not seen and yet believe.*
> (John 20:19–21, 24–9)

In this passage there are three people or groups of people
– each of them says something about attitudes to the
future and how to cope with it.

There are the disciples who were locked into the fear
of a future without Jesus. There is Thomas who seemed
unable to move forward until he was certain of Jesus.
There is Jesus himself, whose presence gives to them all
release from the fear that holds them. Let us look at these
one at a time because they have a powerful message of
freedom for us.

The disciples had travelled around with Jesus during

his ministry. They had seen him dealing with the sick, the poor, the clever and the rich. They must have had high hopes for the future as their rabbi rode into Jerusalem on a donkey and the shouts of praise echoed from the crowd. Then, in the space of a few days, all those hopes for the future crashed. The last supper, the confusion of the arrest, the trial and death of Jesus brought their whole world crashing down around them. Fear gripped them. Confused and frightened they ran away and hid. The future lay in ruins and now they themselves were in fear of their own safety. Twice the passage tells us that the doors of the room were locked. Together the disciples are closed in, not just physically but by their own grief and fear.

Next we notice Thomas who was not with them when Jesus came. His attitude to the future is different and yet equally enslaving. He insists that he will not believe until he actually sees that what the disciples say is true. He is unable to move forward because he wants, as we often do, to know before he trusts; to see before he will move. He wants to know for sure before he will do anything.

Finally, there is Jesus. He releases the disciples from their fear. He does this by coming and standing among them. He is *with them* in their fear. Jesus also speaks to them and his words are 'Peace be with you'. Three times he says these words. He not only speaks but offers the disciples the chance to touch him. His offer is made to Thomas who is not rejected for his lack of faith or his inability to trust the future. To Thomas he gives the chance to touch his hands and side; to see and feel his reality. Jesus makes himself available to Thomas to touch and see and know. For all the disciples it is Christ's presence which transforms their attitude to the future from one of fear to one of joy. Jesus is with them, speaks to them and offers them the chance to touch his life and so be liberated from the fear and grief that enslaved them.

In many ways our situations have parallels with those of
the disciples. From their story we can learn that the way
to freedom from fear of the future is to recognise, as they
did, the transforming presence of Christ. Let us look at
how their story can link up with our own.

We notice that the disciples have been through the
incredibly traumatic experience of seeing the one they
loved most crucified like a common criminal. His death,
so unexpected, shattered their dreams for the future.
Everything fell apart. The future was full of fear and
they remained in hiding and 'the doors of the room were
closed'. Fear of the future can force us like them to 'close
our doors'. It can hem us in, tie us down, keep us
enslaved. We need to be freed from it, the doors broken
down so that we can look it full in the face. What enables
us to do this is the presence of Christ.

We note too that Thomas's fear of the future is all tied
up with needing some form of certainty. He is locked in
by his inability to do anything until he sees. Sometimes
our fear of the future enslaves us as we cannot, or will
not, move until we have certain proof that what we are
about to do is the best thing. The trouble is that sometimes the only way to know if it is the best thing is to
make a move; 'to believe even though we do not see'.
Here we are in the realm of trust. Jesus commends those
who believe, those who step out even though they do not
see. Such trust for the future takes great courage but it
is the way to freedom. Thomas, though, requires some
help along the road to this uncompromising trust in
God's presence. Jesus supplies it. He does not pass
Thomas off as being a faithless disciple anymore than he
will pass us off in the times when we are unable to trust.

Finally, we come to Jesus. He does three things for the
disciples which transform their attitude to the future and
free them from their fear of what it may hold. He stands
among them. In other words he is there, present with
them. It is this presence which so alters their attitude.

The future no longer has any power to drive them into the 'closed room'. From now on they will face it with confidence because they know his presence. The fact that we cannot see Jesus in the same way as they did does not mean that his presence is any less real or that it is in some way diminished. His risen presence stands among us and is with us as we face the future.

The other thing Jesus does is to speak to the disciples. In their closed room, in their fear of what might happen and in the doubt of their frightened hearts he speaks 'Peace be with you'. The future would continue to hold problems and difficulties for them. It will for us. The words of peace spoken by the ever present Christ will not make the difficulties disappear but they will enable us to walk on the way to freedom from the power our fears can have over us. It will not all be sweetness and light but in the darkness, the promise of peace remains.

Jesus encourages Thomas to touch him (though we do not know that Thomas actually did so). The risen Christ is real, he is not a ghost. His presence is with us. Our lives are touched by him and we, if we are open, can know that touch and the reality of it.

The way to freedom from the fear of the future lies in the presence of this living, transforming Christ, who has the power to unlock our doors, to stand with us, to assure us of his peace and to touch our lives. His living presence assures that nothing that can happen in the future can separate us from him.

FOR REFLECTION

1. Place yourself consciously in the presence of God.
2. Think prayerfully about the following questions:
    'The doors were closed in the room where the disciples were.' What is your greatest fear of the future? What 'locks you in'?
    'Unless I can put my hand into his side I refuse to

believe.' How much of the Thomas is there in you – wanting to see before moving in trust for the future?

'Jesus came in and stood among them, "Peace be with you", he said . . . Give me your hand; put it into my side." ' The risen Christ stands with you, speaks to you and makes himself available to you. How does knowing this affect the way you face the future?

3. Read the passage from John again. When you have finished go over the story in your mind. Try to imagine yourself in the room with the disciples. Know that Jesus is with you. Listen to him saying to you 'Peace be with you'. Imagine him making himself available to you to touch him.

PRAYER

Close with a prayer committing your future and any fears you may have about it to God.

You may like to use these words of St Paul as a way of expressing your trust that God offers you a future of freedom with him.

For I am certain of this: neither death nor life, nor angels, nor principalities, nothing already in existence and nothing still to come, nor any power, nor the heights nor the depths, nor any created thing whatever, will be able to come between us and the love of God, known to us in Christ Jesus our Lord.

(Romans 8:38–9)

Freedom in Times of Depression

❖

WHEN ADAM WAS MADE REDUNDANT he felt as though his whole world had fallen apart. He knew himself to be subject to what he called 'mood swings' but the notice of redundancy knocked him for six. Looking back he shouldn't have been surprised. The level of orders had been falling for months and cut-backs had been made in many areas within the firm. No new staff were recruited and Adam's department had already lost several people due to voluntary redundancy. But when it did come, the news was still a shock. Rationally he knew it was nothing personal. He was an excellent worker and had done much to build up the firm over the years. It was simply force of circumstances, the combination of factors over which he and his fellow workers had no control.

The first few weeks seemed odd to Adam. Shock turned to anger and anger to disappointment and disappointment to apathy. Then depression set in. The blackness of feeling useless, a failure, and unable to do anything about it engulfed him. He felt at the mercy of something he was unable to control. To pull himself out of it was asking the impossible. It was not just a case of being unemployed. That was both the tip of the iceberg and the last straw. Depression was something he had known before and he knew the depths of the mental pain to which it could lead him. He would wake up in the morning and the day stretched before him like an obstacle course which had to be negotiated. Nothing seemed to bring him joy any more. He would mooch about the house and then sit for hours curled up in a chair staring into space and longing for the oblivion of sleep, or death. Adam's friends watched helplessly. They could do nothing except be with him. One or two tried to tell him to 'pull himself together', but others knew that if it was as simple as that Adam would have done so long ago.

There seemed no way out. Day succeeded day and the blackness went on.

In the Psalms we have a prayer with which many people who suffer from depression can associate. It vividly portrays the anguish of a sufferer.

> *Yahweh, God of my salvation,*
> *when I cry out to you in the night,*
> *may my prayer reach your presence,*
> *hear my cry for help.*
>
> *For I am filled with misery,*
> *my life is on the brink of Sheol,*
> *already numbered amongst those who sink into*
> *oblivion,*
> *I am as one bereft of strength,*
> *left alone among the dead,*
> *like the slaughtered lying in the grave,*
> *whom you remember no more,*
> *cut off as they are from your protection.*
>
> *You have plunged me to the bottom of the grave,*
> *in the darkness, in the depths;*
> *weighted down by your anger,*
> *kept low by your waves.*

You have deprived me of my friends,
made me repulsive to them,
imprisoned, with no escape;
my eyes are worn out with suffering.
I call to you, Yahweh, all day,
I stretch out my hands to you.

Do you work wonders for the dead,
can shadows rise up to praise you?
Do they speak in the grave of your faithful love,
of your constancy in the place of perdition?
Are your wonders known in the darkness,
your saving justice in the land of oblivion?

But, for my part, I cry to you, Yahweh,
every morning my prayer comes before you;
why, Yahweh, do you rebuff me,
turn your face away from me?

Wretched and close to death since childhood,
I have borne your terrors – I am finished!
Your anger has overwhelmed me,
your terrors annihilated me.

They flood around me all day long,
close in on me all at once.
You have deprived me of friends and companions,
and all that I know is the dark.

(Psalm 88)

This psalm is one of a number of psalms which we call psalms of lament. The psalter has many different types of psalms within it such as psalms of thanksgiving, songs of those on a pilgrimage, royal psalms and hymns. Psalms of lament are sometimes a cry for help from the whole community and sometimes they are the prayer of an individual sufferer. Psalm 88 is probably the latter.

The psalm vividly describes the situation of the sufferer. It is clear that the speaker's experience is so awful that it seems like a living death. He feels the horror of oblivion, of a life without God and without meaning. He is on the brink of Sheol, that place beyond the reach of God's goodness. He is at the end of his tether, at the bottom of the pit, 'in prison and unable to escape'. Although his situation is so desperate and although he feels so abandoned he does still express his despair to God. He does still turn to God to cry out in his need, a cry which has been echoed by many sufferers down the centuries.

The psalmist blames God for his particular situation. He sees his suffering as part of the action of God. To understand this we must realise that the Hebrews believed that it was possible to find God in whatever happened to them, whether bad or good. Suffering was seen as an action of God in chastising his people. This chastisement was always part of God's action to bring the people into a living relationship with him. So it should not surprise us that the psalmist thinks of his affliction as sent by God. What would be uppermost in his mind would be, not the cause of his affliction, but the severity of it. Did God have to go so far in order that the right relationship might be restored?

The psalm ends with a shout of absolute horror. He calls on God but hears nothing. He wants to know 'why, Yahweh, do you rebuff me?'. This affliction is like a flood closing in on him and there is no hope. Usually these psalms of lament end with a note of confidence and hope in God's power to save. Alone among the psalms this prayer gives no such assurance. The psalmist's friends have deserted him. He feels rejected by God. (There is no hint that God will intervene.) His only companion is darkness.

The heartfelt cry of Psalm 88 gives us two clues about

how we can begin to find a glimmer of light in times of depression.

The first is that the psalmist is very free in expressing his distress to God. He is right to do so, that is what God wants. One of the central messages of Christianity is that we are not alone in our suffering. God did not create the world like some sort of gigantic plaything and then sit back in remoteness to watch what would happen to it. In the Incarnation he became intimately involved in his creation and that means he became involved in its suffering. The Cross of Jesus shows just how intimate that involvement is. So, when we cry out to God in our distress we call out, not to a remote God, but to a God who is very near.

The second point is that the psalmist's concern is with how to cope with his distress not with the reason for it. The question 'What have I done to deserve this?' is a natural and human one. It is one that may often be in our minds. There is often no answer to the question. But there's a way of finding freedom in the distress. Torturing ourselves looking for the reason for our predicament is not the way to liberation. What will help us is knowing that no matter how little we may feel it, we are not alone. Knowing that others have trod where we tread and Jesus has been here too can give us what we need – even if it is only to hold on by our fingertips. It is his presence that will bring us our freedom.

FOR REFLECTION AND PRAYER

1. Ask the Holy Spirit to guide you into all peace.
2. Jesus said 'Peace I bequeath to you. My own peace I give you, a peace which the world cannot give, this is my gift to you.'
    What prevents you from knowing the peace of Christ in a real and living way?

When have you felt at the end of your tether? How did you react?

What (or who) helped you discover a new sense of peace?

3. Use the saying of Jesus as your prayer. Say it slowly several times. Allow its words to sink into you. Take your time. If you get distracted say the words again and again. Try to hear Jesus saying this to *you*.

4. When you are ready thank him for his gift of peace in your own words.

Freedom from Oppression

◆━━━◆

WHEN RIKKI RETURNED to his home that evening his mother and younger brothers were in the sitting room watching the T.V.

'Rikki, is that you?' asked his mother.

'Well, it's not Santa Claus.' snapped her son, throwing his sports bag on the floor and going straight upstairs to his room.

'Tea will be ready in ten minutes,' shouted his mother at his retreating back, 'and come down in a better mood.'

Rikki threw himself onto his bed. He would get even with that big-mouthed Lenny if it was the last thing he did. Just because he was black didn't mean he had to suffer the sort of abuse Lenny had doled out on the way home from college. Was it always going to be like this? Was he going to spend the rest of his life apologising for the colour of his skin or having to be twice as good as anyone else before he could get anywhere? Is this what it was all about? He felt like a scapegoat. If anything went wrong he usually got the blame. It was as if some white people wanted to shift the reason for all society's ills onto one section of the community. Deep down he knew he was generalising and that not all white people discriminated against him. Even though he knew that, it did not make the oppression of those who did any the less painful to bear.

Rikki had brains. He had youth and strength and he

had the same rights as any other citizen of this country, yet he felt oppressed and discriminated against. Above all he felt angry. He felt angry because he felt imprisoned. It was not the colour of his skin that oppressed him but the assumptions too many people made about him. Just because he was black they thought he must be lazy, arrogant, violent and untrustworthy. Rikki stood up and looked in the mirror. He gave a wry smile. Discrimination was alive and well. He had seen the results of it in his parents. They were always telling him to be careful, to keep quiet and not to 'rock the boat'. But as Rikki looked at himself in the mirror he knew that he wanted to challenge and confront the discrimination that oppressed him. He wanted to be free to be what he was, an intelligent and caring young man. He wanted to be liberated from the assumptions and attitudes to which he had been condemned by too many people just because he happened to be black.

❮━━━❯

In St Mark's Gospel we have an account of Jesus' challenge to the attitudes and actions of one group of people who were abusing another.

So they reached Jerusalem and Jesus went into the Temple and began driving out the men selling and buying there; he upset the tables of the money changers and the seats of the dove sellers. Nor would he allow anyone to carry anything through the Temple. And he taught them and said, 'Does not Scripture say: My house will be called a house of prayer for all peoples? But you have turned it into a bandits' den.' This came to the ears of the chief priests and the scribes, and they tried to find some way of doing away with him; they were afraid of him because the people were carried away by his teaching. And when evening came he went out of the city.

(Mark 11:15–19)

❮━━━❯

At first sight this account of Jesus driving out the dealers from the Temple seems to be all about his righteous indignation at what was happening and his desire that the poor should not be abused. However, if we look more carefully we see that there is more to it than a surface reading would suggest and that the story is really to do with three things which all have something to say to us about oppression and what we can do about it.

This passage is like the filling in a sandwich. It comes in the middle of a story about a fig tree which was not producing any fruit. The story starts with Jesus on his way to the Temple looking for fruit on a tree and not finding any. Then comes the middle of the sandwich, our passage, about Jesus' actions in the Temple itself. Finally we go back to the fig tree which has now died. Why did Mark insert the story about the Temple into the middle of his account of the fig tree? The Temple is the heart of Jewish life and worship but when Jesus comes to it he finds that it is rather like the fig tree. It is all leaf but no fruit. The outward show gives little sign that there are any fruits of truth and righteousness and justice to be found underneath. What is needed then is for this tree, the Temple, to be 'cleansed'. It needs to produce real fruit and if it does not do so then it deserves to be judged and action needs to be taken against it.

Here is the first important point about our passage. We can and should make judgements about what is and is not just and right. Where the fruits of dignity, justice and peace are absent and all we can see are the barren fig trees of oppression, hatred and justice we are right to take a stand and to know that such atrocities are against the will of God and deserve our condemnation.

When Jesus enters the Temple he enters the Court of the Gentiles. Those who were not Jews were allowed to worship in the Temple but only in the outer court. It was here, in the Court of the Gentiles, that in all probability, Jesus discovered the traders and dealers. We assume that

Jesus' anger was aroused when he saw what was going on and how the profiteering was stripping the poor of what little they had. In fact, Mark says nothing about Jesus' anger and he specifically says that it is both the vendors *and the buyers* who are driven out. So what is Jesus doing? What Jesus seems to be objecting to was the fact that a place which had been created for one purpose was being used for another. The purpose of the building had been 'twisted'. It was created for the worship of God but was now being used for the secular purpose of buying and selling. Even if honest trading was happening the initial and primary purpose of the Temple was being abused. Here is the next important point. Oppression is an abuse of what is good. We are created as unique individuals and, as St Paul says, we ourselves are temples. When human beings who are 'temples of the Holy Spirit' are oppressed, the primary purpose for which God created them is abused. When we suffer from injustice we cannot live in the fullness of life that Christ promised to us. The image of God in which we were created is defiled. The purpose for which people are created is twisted by oppression.

Jesus' action in the Temple has nothing to do with the worship that is going on in the inner courts. His action is confined to one area, that of the buyers and the sellers in the outer courts. *Where* this happens is important. It is the one part of the Temple where Gentiles could enter to worship that was being used as a thoroughfare. Hence Jesus' refusal to 'allow anyone to carry anything through the Temple' (v 16). Jesus' action therefore is not against the worship going on in the Temple itself, it is a condemnation that the Gentiles, who cannot take a full part in that activity, are even being prevented from worshipping in the one area open to them. It is possible that by acting as he did, Jesus is making the point that the Gentiles have rights too. He is safeguarding the rights and privileges of the outsider. By doing so he is championing their rights and proclaiming that they too are created in the image of God and loved by him.

This championing of the outsider, the outcast and the oppressed, is a hallmark of the ministry of Jesus. His stance that everyone has the right to be free regardless of sex, status and race and that each is loved by God is shown by this action in the Temple. By doing so he proclaims that oppression is wrong, has no place in the plan of God, and should be opposed so that all can be free.

The account of Jesus throwing out the buyers and sellers from the Temple says a great deal about our attitude, both to others who are oppressed, and to ourselves when we experience this. Oppression takes many forms. It can come from obvious outside forces where one person in a group harshly treats another, or it can be less overt. We may feel weighed down by our own situation or even by our own temperament, unable to escape from a continual cruelty from within or without which threatens to destroy us. Whatever its form, oppression enslaves us. How then can this passage from St Mark's Gospel help us towards liberation?

First, we noted that Jesus was very forthright about the situation he found. He does not stand on the sidelines and watch what is happening. Rather he confronts it. The way towards freedom does not consist in remaining passive but in facing the oppression, whether it is within ourselves or against others. What we are asked to do is to put a *name* to the problem. Naming it for what it is is the first step to our liberation and to the liberation of others.

Next we noted that oppression is often an abuse or a twisting of what is essentially good. When we are weighed down we are not free to be what God wants us to be. The story tells us that we must try to restore what is good. Where others are concerned this should lead us to positive action. If the oppression is from within we must somehow find a way of letting Jesus restore that diseased part of us where we feel crushed and oppressed. We need to believe that we are created in the image and likeness of God and that is what he loves in us and wishes to restore in us. He will go to endless lengths to work in us to free us.

The story shows above all that Jesus safeguards the rights and the privileges of the outsider, in this case, the Gentiles. His action proclaims that no matter what form the oppression takes, he is with us in our battle to be free from it. His stance shows that no matter who we are, he is there and no matter how we are weighed down he is our champion. Our freedom may not lie in the removal of the cause of our oppression but it will lie in the knowledge that God is *our* God, the God of the poor, of the outcast, of the oppressed. Freedom comes in knowing we have a God who is for us in our battle against all that weighs us down.

FOR REFLECTION

1. Spend a moment consciously bringing yourself into the presence of God.
2. Think about the world in which you live. What forms of oppression do you see? You may like to start by thinking of the whole world and gradually narrow your picture down through our country, our cities, the town or village in which you live, the people you know, and down to your own family and close friends. If it helps, make a list.
3. Spend a moment reflecting on what oppresses you. What effect does it have on the way you feel? What effect does it have on the way you live your life?

PRAYER

In your own words bring your thoughts before God.

Ask him to forgive you for the times you oppress others.

Ask him to give you the courage in the battle to free them and to stand up for what is right.

Ask him to help you be aware of his presence with you in your own situation.

You might like to use the following psalm as a prayer with which to finish.

> Yahweh is my light and my salvation,
> whom should I fear?
> Yahweh is the fortress of my life,
> whom should I dread?
>
> When the wicked advance against me
> to eat me up,
> they, my opponents, my enemies,
> are the ones who stumble and fall.
>
> Though an army pitch camp against me,
> my heart will not fear,
> though war break out against me,
> my trust will never be shaken.
>
> Yahweh, teach me your way,
> lead me on the path of integrity
> because of my enemies;
> do not abandon me to the will of my foes—
> false witnesses have risen against me,
> and are breathing out violence.
>
> This I believe: I shall see the goodness of Yahweh,
> in the land of the living.
> Put your hope in Yahweh, be strong, let your heart
> be bold,
> put your hope in Yahweh.
>
> (Psalm 27:1–3, 11–14)

Freedom from Anger

◆━━━◆

STEPHEN WAS ANGRY. He was angry with himself rather than his sister. How many times had he vowed that he would keep calm and not let Sarah 'get to him'? Somehow his younger sister had this incredible knack of annoying him to the point where, despite all his good intentions, he lost his temper. She didn't mean to do it but, even when they were children, he had often got angry with her and usually got into trouble for it. This time it had been over the toothpaste. It was all so stupid.

'I see you've been squeezing the tube in the middle again,' said Sarah, waving the toothpaste tube at him as he crossed the landing. 'You should squeeze it *from the bottom*.'

'What difference does it make?' replied Stephen, knowing that his sister didn't mean to taunt him.

'It's obvious, squeeze it from the middle and you get a huge dent in it and then you have to fiddle around trying to persuade the stuff to get up to the nozzle. Squeeze it from the bottom and there's no problem. I thought as a computer expert you would be more logical.'

'Logic has nothing to do with it,' retorted Stephen, already feeling his anger about to explode.

'You pride yourself on your logic don't you?'

'I do nothing of the sort.'

And so it had gone on, the toothpaste forgotten as the

argument grew and developed. It had ended with Stephen calling his sister a couple of very unpleasant names.

'Thanks very much,' said Sarah, the look of hurt all too plain on her face. She turned on her heel and went into her room. Helpless to do anything about his own anger and frustration Stephen had walked slowly to the kitchen. Why was he so incapable of freeing himself from this anger and temper which Sarah seemed so easily to bring to the surface. If she got angry in return it might make things easier but she never did. That made him even more cross. Annoyed with her and with himself he made a cup of tea and sat staring into the cup, brooding.

◆━━━◆

In the Book of Jonah we see someone who got very angry. Jonah had been sent by God to tell the people of Nineveh that they should repent. Jonah goes very reluctantly. He tries to run away to Tarshish to escape God's call. Eventually he does what God asks and delivers God's message that the city of Nineveh, renowned for its wickedness, will be overthrown. Having heard the message the people do repent and turn to God. Jonah becomes very angry that God should forgive them so easily when they have been so wicked and he goes off in a sulk. Here is what happens when he sees God is going to forgive the people.

This made Jonah very indignant; he fell into a rage. He prayed to Yahweh and said, 'Please, Yahweh, isn't this what I said would happen when I was still in my own country? That was why I first tried to flee to Tarshish, since I knew you were a tender, compassionate God, slow to anger, rich in faithful love, who relents about inflicting disaster. So now Yahweh, please take my life, for I might as well be dead as go on living.' Yahweh replied, 'Are you right to be angry?'

Jonah then left the city and sat down to the east of the city. There he made himself a shelter and sat under

it in the shade to see what would happen to the city.
Yahweh God then ordained that a castor-oil plant should
grow up over Jonah to give shade for his head and soothe
his ill-humour; Jonah was delighted with the castor-oil
plant. But at dawn the next day, God ordained that a
worm should attack the castor-oil plant – and it with-
ered. Next, when the sun rose, God ordained that there
should be a scorching east wind; the sun beat down so
hard on Jonah's head that he was overcome and begged
for death, saying, 'I might as well be dead as go on
living.' God said to Jonah, 'Are you right to be angry
about the castor-oil plant?' He replied, 'I have every right
to be angry, mortally angry!' Yahweh replied, 'You are
concerned for the castor-oil plant which has not cost you
any effort and which you did not grow, which came up
in a night and has perished in a night. So why should I
not be concerned for Nineveh, the great city, in which
there are more than a hundred and twenty thousand
people who cannot tell their right hand from their left,
to say nothing of all the animals?'

(Jonah 4)

The whole of this book is designed to help the reader see
that God has no favourites, that his love is for everyone.
It is an astonishingly broad-minded God that we see in
these four chapters.

It is difficult for us to imagine the impact this story
would have had on its original hearers. It was written
quite late in Israel's history and the people were tempted
to withdraw into a narrow, almost racist, view of themselves and their relations with other people. Nineveh
represents Israel's detested enemy. They represented
everything that seemed against God. They were pagan,
wicked, and of another race to the people of Israel. Yet
here is God, not only appealing that they repent, but
actually forgiving these notorious evil doers. It is this

unconditional love of God that knows no boundaries that causes Jonah to become so angry. After all, is not he an Israelite, one of the chosen? Had not his people, despite their failures and disobedience, been the ones with whom God had developed a special relationship? How could God just let these others off; these outsiders who knew nothing of the God of Israel? Seeing how God is forgiving these people Jonah feels he has every right to be angry. They had done nothing to earn this forgiveness. It was unfair, unjust and unforgivable of God to act in this unconditional way. The picture we have of God then is of infinite compassion. As Jonah himself says, it is a God who is slow to anger, rich in faithful love, who relents about inflicting disaster.

If we look more closely at Jonah himself we see the irony in the story. It is not the pagans nor the notorious sinners who come across as the most unlikeable but Jonah himself. It is the Israelite; the prophet called by God who is so priggish. All the Gentiles, the sailors, even the humble Ninevites come across as very likeable characters. Jonah sulks, gets angry, is rebellious and is generally the most disagreeable of all the people pictured.

It is this miserable, angry and priggish character that God gently leads to new understanding.

The story of Jonah and his anger at what he thinks is the justice of God's action has a message for us. As we seek to be freed from our own anger we can learn several important lessons from this passage.

Accepting anger ourselves. The first thing to notice is that God does not dismiss Jonah's anger. He knows only too well that Jonah is furious. He also understands the reasons for it. It is vital that we realise that we cannot dismiss our anger or pretend it does not matter or that it is not there. Nothing is gained by suppressing or pretending. This does not mean that we have the right to 'let fly' whenever we wish, but it does mean that we should be open enough to see what is really happening to us. If we realise that God does not dismiss our anger then we too should be able to face this part of ourselves.

God accepts our anger. The second point to notice is that God actually accepts Jonah's anger. He is very gentle with this wayward prophet of his. Jonah is not thrown aside by God because he gets cross at what is happening, in fact the exact opposite occurs. God goes to great lengths to explain to Jonah what he has done for the Ninevites and why he has done it. Quite rightly we are unhappy with our inability to control all our outbursts of anger. However, failure to cope does not mean that God treats us any differently from the way he treated Jonah. He is as understanding and gentle and accepting with us as he was with his angry prophet. Indeed, as with Jonah, God will go to great lengths to help us to come to terms with what is happening to us.

God uses our anger. The third thing to notice is that God uses Jonah's situation to lead him into new understanding. It is not just that God accepts Jonah's anger, he uses it. God uses what seems an impossible and negative emotion to give Jonah, and the people Jonah represents, a new understanding of the sort of God he is.

So far we have looked at how God acted with regard to Jonah's anger. What we do not know is how Jonah reacted to God. The book simply finishes with God stating what he has done. Whether Jonah learnt from what had happened to him and whether or not he was able to accept that God's love was for everyone is left unfinished. Coming to terms with a new idea can create many conflicting emotions within us. Fear, uncertainty, confusion and anger can all be present as we work out how to react to a changed idea or a changed circumstance. The way to freedom from anger is not to pretend it does not exist. It is to learn the lesson of Jonah. It is to realise that God knows it is there, accepts it for what it is and can use it to bring good out of something so inherently destructive.

In our own lives the open question is whether or not we shall react to God working within us to free us. It is as open a question as whether or not Jonah himself learnt his lesson.

FOR REFLECTION

1. Spend some time placing yourself in the presence of God.
2. Ask him to help you to be open with him.
3. Think about the times when you get angry. What makes you angry? Why do you get angry? How often do you get angry?
4. Bring each of the situations you have thought about into the presence of God. In your own words ask him to forgive you the hurt you have done to others, to yourself and to him.
5. Read the story from Jonah again.
6. Ask yourself, are you as open with God about your anger as Jonah was? Do you really believe God loves and accepts you, all of you including your anger? Do you really believe that God can use your anger and the negative forces within you to teach you more about yourself and about him? Do you really believe that God has the power to help you handle your anger?

PRAYER

Bring your thoughts before God in your own words. Ask that you may be aware of his love and his power to free you.

You may like to use these words if you cannot find your own.

> Listen to me, Yahweh, answer me,
> for I am poor and needy.

Guard me, for I am faithful,
save your servant who relies on you.

Lord, you are kind and forgiving,
rich in faithful love for all who call upon you.
Yahweh, hear my prayer,
listen to the sound of my pleading.

(Psalm 86:1–2, 5–6)

Freedom from Sin

❖

YOU COULD HARDLY describe Alan as a tearaway. He worked as a clerk in a bank and went fishing at the weekends. Other people liked Alan. He was good fun yet dependable, ready to share a joke yet with a serious side to him. Even though he had not really enjoyed school much he had done reasonably well and had never 'been in trouble'. Yet Alan was very conscious of his own failings and in particular of his tendency to 'use people'. It was not that he was particularly rude but deep down he knew that if it came to the crunch he would always put himself first. If he wanted something badly enough he would go all out to get it, no matter what he had to do or who he had to trample over in the process. Alan did not like this side of his nature. Most of the time it was not too much of a problem but he saw it surfacing in little ways, in his relationships at work and at home.

Coping with this desire always to put himself first was difficult for Alan. He felt enslaved by his selfishness and unable to do much about it. Furthermore he did not seem to be improving. Rather he saw the tendency asserting itself more often. That it was wrong to be so self-centred Alan had no doubt. Deep down he longed to be free enough to give himself to others regardless of the cost and to put others first even if it resulted in giving up his own place in the pecking order. Yet his longing to be

free from what he knew was sinful seemed never to be
fulfilled.

What made the situation even worse was Alan's awareness that his failures hurt other people. He knew that his
actions, words and attitude caused misery to those he
trampled over or simply ignored. They were paying the
price for his wrongdoing.

In the Book of Hosea we have the words of a prophet
who knew from personal experience what it meant to be
sinned against. Here is what he said about God's reaction
to his wayward people.

When Israel was a child I loved him,
and I called my son out of Egypt.
But the more I called the further they went away from
    me;
and offered sacrifice to Baal
and burnt incense to idols.
I myself taught Ephraim to walk,
I myself took them by the arm,
but they did not know that I was the one caring for
    them,
that I was leading them with human ties,
with leading-strings of love,
that, with them, I was like someone lifting an infant
    to his cheek,
and that I bent down to feed him.

Ephraim how could I part with you?
Israel, how could I give you up?
How could I make you like Admah
or treat you like Zeboiim?
My heart within me is overwhelmed,
fever grips my inmost being.
I will not give rein to my fierce anger,

I will not destroy Ephraim again,
for I am God, not man,
the Holy One in your midst,
and I shall not come to you in anger.

(Hosea 11:1–4, 8–9)

◆━━━◆

Hosea prophesied during the eighth century BC along with Amos, Micah and First Isaiah. Amos had a stern message for the people, denouncing them for their sin and proclaiming that God had had enough of their social injustice. It is a dark picture which Amos paints of God's judgement and righteous indignation. Hosea too castigates the people but he has a tone of gentleness which we do not find in Amos, perhaps because of his own personal grief.

The original Hebrew text is often unclear, but we think that Hosea had an unfaithful wife, Gomer. It was this unhappy marriage which led him to talk about God's relationship with his people in a similar way. Israel was like Gomer, an unfaithful wife to God who had given her everything. He had taken her as his own in the desert but she had gone her own way and 'played the harlot'. She had betrayed God's trust and sinned against him.

In this passage the prophet gives us what is one of the greatest expositions of the depths of God's love in the Old Testament. In it he pictures God as the father of wayward children, unable to give them up no matter what they had done or how unfaithful they had been. This magnificent passage gives us the assurance that no matter how far we have gone from God he always remains faithful to us. Let us look at it a little more closely to see how it can help us to be free from the awareness of our sinfulness and failures.

First we see that God is only too aware of what Israel had done. He had called them out of the desert and made a special relationship with them, a covenant, but the closer he came to them the more they turned away from him. God knows quite well the sin of his people, the depth and horror of it.

Next we glimpse the depth to which the unfaithfulness had gone. God carried his people and like a Father taught them to walk (the image is that of the harness used to help young children learn to walk). He lifts them close to him and feeds them yet they remain in their unfaithfulness. Despite all this loving care they have gone away. It only adds to the awfulness of what they have done.

Then we read of God's longing for them. We can almost feel the heartbreak of the cry 'how could I part with you'. No matter what they have done God cannot give them up. It is almost a lament over a people who have failed to see the depths of God's love and failed to recognise how limitless that love is.

Finally we see that, although God is holy, just and righteous it is his mercy and love which will be shown to the people. He will not come to them in anger. It is mercy not condemnation that will be shown. God's love is endless and he gives it freely.

This beautiful passage offers us a glimpse into the way God deals with us and the way to find freedom from the results of our own waywardness.

Loved to the end. The first and most important message of this passage for us is that no matter what we have done, or how far we have travelled away from what we know to be right, God still loves us. It is a resounding call to believe that the love of God is infinite and that however unfaithful we are, we are never beyond the embrace of that love. He knows quite well the depth and horror of our failures and sin but that does not stop him from loving us. It is his love and our awareness of the depths of it that gives us confidence to turn to him and be freed.

God's longing. We also see in this passage the longing of

God that we should 'come home'. He has been with us all the time, he laments over our desire to do our own thing and he longs for us to turn around and recognise him. His anguished cry of longing over Israel is addressed to us too. 'How could I part with you?' That God should long for us so intensely and will never give up on us even if we are tempted to give up on ourselves should prevent us from falling into despair. Responding to that longing and knowing the depth of it enables us to be picked up by God each time we fall and to know he is a God of endless patience.

God's mercy. Finally the depths of God's longing and of the love it shows, gives us a picture of a merciful God. This mercy does not mean that God condones our sin or is not indignant about it. What it means is that we can have confidence that, when we turn to him, it is not his anger that will be shown to us but his mercy. It is knowing that God's tender love, like that of a Father pictured by Hosea, and his infinite compassion outweighs all our sin and enables us to keep starting again. We may get discouraged, we may feel we shall never be free of our inbuilt tendency to move away from God and what he wishes, but this passage assures us that God stays with us. His love and his mercy lead us and the path is towards freedom.

FOR REFLECTION

1. Spend some time in quiet and remember God is with you.
2. Think through the last few days. When have you known yourself to be thinking, speaking or acting in a way that is sinful? How do you feel about what has happened?
3. Picture Jesus sitting by the Sea of Galilee. He is alone. You go up to him and he smiles. You sit beside him.

He asks you to tell him what you have been thinking
about. What do you say? What does he say to you?

PRAYER

Close with a prayer of your own or use these words from
Psalm 103.

Bless Yahweh, my soul,
from the depths of my being, his holy name;
bless Yahweh my soul,
never forget all his acts of kindness.

He forgives all your offences,
cures all your diseases,
he redeems your life from the abyss,
crowns you with faithful love and tenderness;
he contents you with good things all your life,
renews your youth like an eagle's.

Yahweh acts with uprightness,
with justice to all who are oppressed;
he revealed to Moses his ways,
his great deeds to the children of Israel.

Yahweh is tenderness and pity,
slow to anger and rich in faithful love;
his indignation does not last for ever,
nor his resentment remain for all time;
he does not treat us as our sins deserve,
nor repay us as befits our offences.

As the height of heaven above earth,
so strong is his faithful love for those who fear him.
As the distance of east from west,
so far from us does he put our faults.

As tenderly as a father treats his children,
so Yahweh treats those who fear him;
he knows of what we are made,
he remembers that we are dust.

(Psalm 103:1–14)

Freedom from Guilt

◀▬▬▶

FOUR YEARS AGO Craig announced to his mother that he was not going anywhere near a church anymore. Sheila could hardly say she was surprised. She had noticed his resentment and unwillingness for months and months. She had suspected he was only going along to please her and Tom. She had tried different ways to prevent him from 'lapsing' but neither the gentle nudging and questioning nor the firm-handed approach had worked. She had just about got to the point of believing she had done her best for him, and that he was a responsible adult and must make his own decisions, when he told her he had found a flat to rent. He was moving into it with his current girlfriend. It was then that they had their blazing row. That day Sheila said much she was later to regret. Many harsh words were shouted, unkind accusations were thrown around. In the end Craig had walked from the house vowing he would never return; a vow he had kept for four long years.

Sheila tried to convince herself that her anger was righteous indignation but deep down she knew it was an expression of bitter disappointment and not a little guilt. 'It's all my fault,' she said to Tom, 'if I had brought him up better this wouldn't have happened. If only I had kept my temper, if only I had listened.' No matter how she tried to convince herself that Craig was an independent young man, that she had done her best, she was still beset by guilt. She felt guilty because she thought she had failed him and guilty because she had created a situation which she suspected could never be put right. It was all her fault that he never wanted to come home again. She had driven him away.

Everyone feels guilty at some time or other. There are times when we all do or say things of which we are ashamed; things we know to be wrong. It is good we *do* feel guilty about these things because guilt reminds us that what we have done, or not done, is a failure on our part to love unselfishly as God loves. When we have a pain in our body it tells us that something needs attending to. Guilt can be like a nerve ending telling us that there is something wrong with us that needs to be put right. But God does not want us to go on feeling guilty anymore than he wants us to go on feeling pain. Guilt can enslave us. It can be very destructive. Like some sort of hungry beast it can slowly eat away at us. How can we be free from the guilt that holds us captive?

In St Luke's Gospel we have the story of a woman who knows only too well what it is to be enslaved by guilt.

One of the Pharisees invited him to a meal. When he arrived at the Pharisee's house and took his place at table, suddenly a woman came in, who had a bad name in the town. She had heard he was dining with the Pharisee and had brought with her an alabaster jar of ointment. She waited behind him at his feet, weeping, and her tears fell on his feet, and she wiped them away with her hair; then she covered his feet with kisses and anointed them with the ointment.

When the Pharisee who had invited him saw this, he said to himself, 'If this man were a prophet, he would know who this woman is and what sort of a person it is who is touching him and what a bad name she has.'

Then Jesus took him up and said, 'Simon, I have some-
thing to say to you.' He replied, 'Say on, Master.' 'There
was once a creditor who had two men in his debt; one
owed him five hundred denarii, the other fifty. They were
unable to pay, so he let them both off. Which of them
will love him more?' Simon answered, 'The one who was
let off more, I suppose.' Jesus said, 'You are right.'

Then he turned to the woman and said to Simon, 'You
see this woman? I came into your house, and you poured
no water over my feet, but she has poured out her tears
over my feet and wiped them away with her hair. You
gave me no kiss, but she has been covering my feet with
kisses ever since I came in. You did not anoint my head
with oil, but she has anointed my feet with ointment.
For this reason I tell you that her sins, many as they are,
have been forgiven her, because she has shown such
great love. It is someone who is forgiven little who shows
little love. Then he said to her, 'Your sins are forgiven.'
(Luke 7:36–48)

This is one of the many stories in the Gospels about Jesus
freeing people from inner pain. It is a lovely story about
the forgiveness of God which frees a woman from the
guilt she feels about the past and the new hope he gives
her for the future.

In the story the woman comes to Jesus very aware of
what she has done. There is a special place for people
such as her in Luke's Gospel. He seems to have a special
understanding and feeling for outcasts and sinners. He
shows Jesus reacting with gentleness and understanding
towards such people. Characteristically Luke does not
tell us this woman's name. There is no good reason for
thinking she is Mary Magdalene or Mary the sister of
Martha. The fact that she remains anonymous does not
really matter because there is a sense in which she is all
of us. We can see ourselves so clearly in her.

Whoever she was she certainly had a bad reputation in her community. Probably she was a prostitute. If not, she may have been married to someone who was an outcast or a 'sinner'. Whatever she had done she knew what it was to feel guilty and to long for a new start.

Apart from Jesus, there are two main characters to notice in this story. First, of course, there is the woman, then there is Simon. Let us look at the woman. She shows us three things.

First, this woman knows her *needs*. She knows her emptiness and the way her past is enslaving her. She experiences what we so often experience, a longing to be free of the guilt caused by knowing we have done wrong. Perhaps she felt, as we do, that we have not only failed God but that we have failed to live up to the standards we set ourselves.

Second, this woman knows that Jesus can *meet these needs*. She seems instinctively to realise that he can do something for her. Indeed her tears may well be tears, not of sorrow, but of gratitude for the freedom his love brings her.

Thirdly, this woman comes to Jesus in *total abandonment*. She could not have known for certain when she entered Simon's home what Jesus' reaction would be. If she had seen his dealings with other people she would have been pretty sure that he would accept her but could she be certain? I doubt it. So, she comes in sheer trust and makes this beautiful act of homage.

Now let us take a look at the second person in the story, Simon the Pharisee. We do not know why Simon invited Jesus for a meal. It may be that he simply wished to meet him and to learn from him. It may be that he wished to show Jesus off to his friends by inviting this wandering teacher to his home. It may be that he had ideas of trapping Jesus into making a statement that could be used against him.

Whatever reasons Simon had for inviting Jesus his

welcome is one of respect and courtesy. However, Jesus does not find a really warm welcome in Simon's home. When the woman arrives and begins to act in what Simon thought was a very improper manner, he is full of righteous indignation and judges Jesus' reaction to the woman in a very critical way. 'If this man were a prophet he would know who this woman is and what sort of person it is who is touching him and what a bad name she has.' Naturally, he does not voice this criticism out loud but says it 'to himself'. In some ways the picture we get of Simon is the opposite to that of the woman.

First, we saw how the woman comes to Jesus very aware of her needs. Simon does not appear to be aware of any need in himself, he sees only too clearly the failure of this woman, and the guilt she feels, but he does not see his own. He fails to see that in setting himself up as her judge he is committing a sin himself. He is blind to his own need for forgiveness because he does not see that he really has anything much to forgive. He seems to have no feelings of guilt to be freed from.

Secondly, we also saw how this woman, aware of her need, knew that Jesus could do something about it. Simon cannot do this because Simon is a model of self-sufficiency. He has everything sewn up. He has religion neatly in a box and he has God sorted out too. How can he believe that Jesus has the power to liberate when he does not know what he needs liberating from?

Thirdly, we saw how this woman in her anguish totally abandons herself to Jesus. She shows such trust and faith. Self-sufficient Simon has no need of all this. No doubt he thought this person an 'emotional woman'. Yet, in this self-sufficiency of Simon's there is one big flaw. There is something lacking. What is lacking is warmth and a willingness to admit need. Simon is presented as a 'closed up' person. There does not seem to be any warmth in him. His welcome is guarded, he voices criticism to himself, his reply to Jesus' question is correct, but it is given grudgingly. Somehow it is difficult to imagine Simon throwing himself on the mercy and trust of Jesus in the abandonment of trust and faith. Self-sufficient people rarely can.

The final person in the story is Jesus himself. He respects both people. To Simon he administers a rebuke in the form of a story but he does so in a way that makes Simon think things out for himself. We get the impression that Jesus is trying to move Simon on in his thinking and to help him see that this woman has great need and great love.

To the woman Jesus shows understanding and compassion. By the very way he treats her he shows that he respects her dignity, no matter what the past has been or the guilt she feels about it. Jesus only speaks to this woman once but when he does he releases more than words; he releases a liberating force that enables her and the many thousands of people like her to find freedom from the awareness of failure and guilt. 'Your sins are forgiven'. They are spoken to us too with the same promise of freedom.

There is something of a Simon and something of the woman in each of us. Jesus has the power to liberate us from our guilt but we have to be like the woman. Like her, we have to recognise our need, believe that he can act and trust him to do so. But there is a great deal of the Simon in us too. We want to deal with our failures and guilt ourselves and we sometimes half believe that such a total abandonment to God is a sign of weakness. In reality, failure and the guilt that comes from it, are not the obstacles to our discovery of the freedom Jesus offers. The obstacle is our own self-sufficiency. Failure, sin, weakness and guilt can all be dealt with by God but he can do nothing for the self-sufficient because self-sufficiency blocks all his advances. It is when we admit our needs and open ourselves to him, like this woman, that his love can liberate us from the guilt that has the power to destroy us.

FOR REFLECTION

1. Spend some time placing yourself in the presence of God.
2. Ask him to help you to be open to him.
3. Read the story from St Luke's Gospel again.
4. Ask yourself: Who am I most like in this story, Simon or the woman? What do I feel guilty about? Do I believe God can free me from the guilt I feel? How self-sufficient am I?

PRAYER

Bring your thoughts before God in your own words. Ask that you may be aware of his love and his power to free you from any guilt you feel about your past failures. You may like to use these words if you cannot find your own.

Father, I believe you want me to know the freedom
    living in your presence brings.
Release me from worry about my past failures.
Free me from the guilt I feel.
Help me to trust in your love and forgiveness so that I
    may begin each day afresh in the sure and certain
    knowledge of your love for me.

Freedom in Times of Pain

———◄══►———

IT HAD STARTED, with a severe bout of flu. Michelle seemed to be taking a long time to get over it. She would spend hours doing nothing but sleeping. It was as much as she could do to get out of bed and downstairs. She would lie on the settee for hours unable to do anything. Sometimes when her husband, Andrew, returned from work in the evening he would find her in almost the same position on the settee as when he had left that morning. It was as much as she could do to make herself a cup of tea.

At first the doctor had said that in due time Michelle would be back to normal but as time went on this was clearly not the case. She didn't seem to improve at all. The days turned into weeks and the weeks into months until eventually ME was diagnosed. Myalgic encephalomyelitis, acute post-viral fatigue, is not life-threatening, but it was going to be long slow process back to normality.

It was not just her physical condition that Michelle found hard to bear. It was the attitude of those around her. To begin with she found that people just did not understand. She had not got the energy or the inclination to try and explain it to them. But their misunderstanding about her condition; their belief that she was malingering added to her physical discomfort. So, added to her ME was the mental anguish of trying to cope with people who could not, or would not, understand the reason why an active woman should suddenly be reduced to such passivity.

Worse than the misunderstanding was the sniping. People began to treat her as if she were a leper or as if it was all her fault. Sometimes when people came to visit the house they would simply talk over her addressing all their questions about her to her husband. It was as if she was a non-person; as if she did not exist anymore. Sometimes they would try to bully her out of her condition, telling her to 'pull her socks up' and to 'make the best of what she had'.

Andrew was wonderful. He tried his best to support and care for his wife but no matter how much he told her that her condition was not her fault and that she, as a person, was more important to him than anything else in the world it did not soothe the pain. She felt as if she was only living half a life and as if all the joy had gone out from it. She felt enslaved, not just by her physical illness but also by what it was doing to her as a person. Sometimes she would sit and look out of the window watching the children playing. She would watch them run and chase each other across the park remembering her own youth and vitality that had now been taken from her. Watching their exuberance only made the pain seem even worse. How she wished that she could rush out there and join them and how she wished too, that she could be freed from the mental anguish that her illness was causing her.

◆━━━▶

In the Books of Samuel we have a description of a woman in pain. Hannah was one of the two wives of Elkanah. She had never been able to have children.

One day Elkanah offered a sacrifice. Now he used to give portions to Peninnah and to all her sons and daughters;

*to Hannah, however, he would give only one portion:
for, although he loved Hannah more, Yahweh had made
her barren. Furthermore, her rival would taunt and provoke her, because Yahweh had made her womb barren.
And this went on year after year; every time they went
up to the temple of Yahweh she used to taunt her. On
that day she wept and would not eat anything; so her
husband Elkanah said, 'Hannah, why are you crying?
Why are you not eating anything? Why are you so sad?
Am I not more to you than ten sons?'*

*When they had finished eating in the room, Hannah
got up and stood before Yahweh. Eli the priest was sitting
on his seat by the doorpost of the temple of Yahweh. In
the bitterness of her soul she prayed to Yahweh with
many tears . . .*

*While she went on praying to Yahweh, Eli was
watching her mouth, for Hannah was speaking under
her breath; her lips were moving but her voice could not
be heard, and Eli thought she was drunk. Eli said, 'How
much longer are you going to stay drunk? Get rid of your
wine.' 'No, my lord,' Hannah replied, 'I am a woman in
great trouble; I have not been drinking wine or strong
drink – I am pouring out my soul before Yahweh. Do
not take your servant for a worthless woman; all this
time I have been speaking from the depth of my grief
and my resentment.' Eli then replied, 'Go in peace, and
may the God of Israel grant what you have asked of him.'*

(I Samuel 1:4–10, 12–17)

<hr>

When this story opens Hannah is the childless wife of
Elkanah. We know that later she is to become the mother
of Samuel, that great prophet who anointed Saul, the first
King of Israel. Hannah is not the only woman in the Bible
who is childless but who then has a son who grows up
to be an important figure in the history of God's dealings
with his people. The mothers of Isaac, Samson, and John

the Baptist are all said to be barren. Barrenness was seen as a real affliction at that time. Not to be able to have children, and particularly a son, was one of the worst things that could happen to a woman.

In this passage we have the very human story of what this mental anguish meant to Hannah. First of all we read that the family had gone to Shiloh on pilgrimage. Possibly this was for the Feast of Shelters, or the Feast of Tabernacles about which we read in the New Testament. Shiloh was an important place and the pilgrimage there would have been one of great joy. It ended with a sacrificial meal, the mood of which was one of great joy and gaiety. It is in this context when everyone is cheerful and joyful that Hannah pours out her problems before God. It is almost as if the atmosphere of gladness heightens her own anguish. Secondly we notice that Peninnah, Elkanah's other wife, resorts to taunting Hannah because she is barren. The rather casual reference to polygamy probably indicates that it was acceptable at the time and it may have grown out of the need to continue the line and what would happen if one wife proved to be childless. We have other examples in the situation of Abraham and Jacob. The same sort of rivalry also exists between two women in the case of Abraham. It is clear however, in our passage, that Eli loves Hannah greatly but no matter how much he loves her the taunts of Peninnah go deep. Such attitudes only add to the pain.

It is not only Peninnah that increases the anguish Hannah feels, for when she does pour out her heart to God at the door of the temple, Eli, the priest, misunderstands what she is doing. It was unusual to pray silently so when Eli sees Hannah's lips moving but hears no words he assumes that she is drunk. Without giving her a chance to defend herself he castigates her. It is to Eli's credit that he immediately recognises his mistake. Hannah has enough trouble with her own condition and her relationship with Peninnah without finding that she is being prevented from pouring out her heart to God as well.

Hannah's situation is clearly one which she can do nothing about. We know that the taunts of Peninnah had gone on year after year. The bearing of the insults as well as the condition itself seemed unresolvable. Hannah was trapped both by her own physical inability to have children and by the misunderstandings and the taunts of those around her. To all intents and purposes it seemed there was no way out.

Elkanah, her husband, does his best in this intolerable situation. We read that he loves her greatly and that, when all is joyful at the feast, he does his best to sooth her yet, despite the comfort this must have brought her, it does not free her from her situation.

This story has elements with which it is easy to associate. It is a very human story and has many of the elements that enable us to identify with it in times of suffering. Hannah's reaction to her physical condition and to the mental anguish that was caused to her by other people because of it, give us a clue to the way we might also begin to walk towards freedom when we are in times of pain, physical or mental.

Coming to terms with pain. First we note that Hannah recognised her situation for what it was. That did not mean that she somehow accepted her suffering without cost. Acceptance of suffering does not mean passivity or fatalism, that 'what will be, will be'. Acceptance is a very positive recognition of what is happening to us; an attempt to make some sort of sense of the pain we are enduring. This does not mean that we will cease to question why it has happened to us or cease to be angry about it, or to run the gamut of a thousand other emotions. Acceptance is simply a coming to terms that this *has* happened and that somehow we must find a way of coping with it.

Sharing pain with others. Hannah's condition was not helped by the attitude of other people. It is wonderful when those around us are like Elkanah, full of love and concern. Their presence enables us to walk towards some sort of freedom from our situation. In their love and care we can relax. We can let them shoulder the burden and for a while, perhaps, to share the pain with us. Such a sharing of the pain does indeed help us towards the healing process. However, our mental anguish can sometimes be made worse when people misunderstand us or taunt us, as happened with Hannah. There are some forms of pain and suffering which are not easy to see and it is people who have to cope with this sort of suffering who often know that it is increased by those who tell them to 'pull up their socks', or that it's time they 'pulled themselves together'. Even if such people do grasp that it is not as simple as that, they are not always as ready as Eli to admit that they have been wrong. It is at times like these especially that those who do understand and those who stay with us are doubly precious. For they can reaffirm us and reassure us that what is happening to us is not our fault. We are not to blame. Our inability to change the situation must not lead us into feeling guilty.

Sharing the pain with God. There is no answer to the problem of pain. We may be fortunate enough to discover that it can teach us things we might not have learnt in any other way but this does not remove its potency or its anguish. For some there is no release until death. But this message does assure us that we are not alone and it is in this knowing that we are not alone that the walk towards freedom lies. Knowing God is with us and that his love is shown through the care and concern of others who share the burden with us will not remove the pain but will perhaps help us not to be enslaved by it.

FOR REFLECTION

1. Spend a moment placing yourself in the presence of God.
2. Slowly and prayerfully read the following passage:

    When the sixth hour came there was darkness over the whole land until the ninth hour and at the ninth hour Jesus cried out in a loud voice, *'Eloi, eloi, lama sabachthani'*, which means, *'My God, My God, why have you forsaken me?'*

                                                    (Mark 15:33–34)

    When have you felt that God had deserted you? What helped you to find him again?
3. Name before God, the people who have helped you in your times of suffering. Thank him for them.
4. Name before God those you know who are suffering now. Pray that they may be able to express their grief before God as Hannah did and may know the strength and assurance of his presence with them.

PRAYER

You may like to close with a prayer of your own or with the following either for yourself or on behalf of someone you know who is suffering.

    My God, my God, why have you forsaken me?
    The words of my groaning do nothing to save me.
    My God, I call by day but you do not answer,
    at night, but I find no respite.

    My strength is trickling away,
    my bones are all disjointed,
    my heart has turned to wax,
    melting inside me.

My mouth is dry as earthenware,
my tongue sticks to my jaw.
You lay me down in the dust of death.

Yahweh, do not hold aloof!
My strength, come quickly to my help.

(Psalm 22:1–2, 14–15, 19)

Freedom in Times of Bereavement

◆━━━◆

WHEN JACK HAD DIED, Kathleen went to pieces. At least it seemed that way to her although others said she managed remarkably well. Jack and Kathleen had been married for fifty-one years and they had been devoted to each other. For the last ten years or so they had been inseparable. Almost every waking moment was spent in each other's company. Kathleen had always taken care of Jack, especially during the last months of his illness when she had nursed him day and night. Now he was gone. A great big hole had appeared in her life where Jack had once been. A hole that could never be filled again.

At first Kathleen had simply been numb. There were things to do. The funeral had to be arranged and she had to sort things out. It all seemed so unreal. The family rallied round and there were people with her most of the time. The sense of unreality stayed with her until after the funeral. She couldn't really take in what had happened. She kept thinking she would walk in and find Jack sitting in his old armchair. She found herself talking about him as if he were still alive. Then she began to clear out his things. It was when she was packing up a box of his shoes that she broke down. Shoes were such personal things, no one else's looked quite like his, moulded as they were to the shape of his feet. She sat on the

edge of the bed, cradling them in her arms, the tears
pouring down her cheeks. Kathleen had always said that
she 'wanted to go first'. Jack had always been far more
resilient than her. He would have coped much better
with bereavement than she could. She felt angry that
he had gone before her; an anger she could not really
rationalise. She felt guilty too as she remembered the
times they had argued and verbally hurt each other. How
she longed to see him once more simply to say sorry and
to tell him of her love for him. She felt that she would
never be able to live again, that with his passing her life
too had ended. Her remaining years would be those of
existence rather than living.

◄══════►

In St John's Gospel we have the story of another woman's
grief over the death of someone she cared about.

*But Mary was standing outside near the tomb, weeping.
Then, as she wept, she stooped to look inside, and saw
two angels in white sitting where the body of Jesus had
been, one at the head, the other at the feet. They said,
'Woman, why are you weeping?' 'They have taken my
Lord away,' she replied, 'and I don't know where they
have put him.' As she said this she turned around and
saw Jesus standing there, though she did not realise that
it was Jesus. Jesus said to her, 'Woman, why are you
weeping? Who are you looking for?' Supposing him to be
the gardener, she said 'Sir, if you have taken him away,
tell me where you have put him, and I will go and
remove him.' Jesus said, 'Mary!' She turned round and
said to him in Hebrew, 'Rabbuni!' – which means
Master. Jesus said to her, 'Do not cling to me, because I
have not yet ascended to the Father. But go to the
brothers and tell them: I am ascending to my Father
and your Father, to my God and your God.' So Mary of*

*Magdala told the disciples 'I have seen the Lord,' and
that he had said these things to her.*

(John 20:11–18)

◆━━━━━◆

The story of Mary of Magdela's grief in the garden has a
number of elements which can help us as we come to
terms with bereavement. Mary had stood by and watched
Jesus die on the cross. We know this from the account
in John 19:25. She had seen the agony of his death and
knew the reality of it. As a last act of love she had gone
to the tomb early on the next day to anoint his body.
When she arrived there she found it empty and immediately went to tell Simon Peter and the other disciples
that someone had removed the body. Like Mary of
Bethany, who lamented the loss of her brother, Lazarus,
this Mary was grief-stricken. She remained in the garden
distraught that, not only had death taken Jesus from her,
even his body had disappeared. There was a very real
sense in which she was searching for Jesus, not in some
spiritual way, but for the body that should have been
in the tomb. In a way, she symbolised the Christian
community for whom John was writing as they, too, were
searching, but their search was for faith.

Mary saw Jesus standing in the garden but did not
recognise him. The inability to recognise Jesus occurs
more than once in the resurrection narratives in St John.
The beloved disciple failed to recognise Jesus on the
beach. Similarly the two disciples on the road to Emmaus
did not see who it was that walked with them. John
wished to stress that it took time for them to recognise
the risen Christ. For John, the mere sight of the risen
Jesus did not mean that there was understanding. It was
quite possible to see and yet not to believe. In John's
Gospel many people see only what is on the surface and
never the reality that lies behind it.

For Mary, recognition came when Jesus spoke her

name. John talked earlier in his Gospel about Jesus calling his sheep, 'The sheep hear his voice, and one by one
he calls his own sheep and leads them out.' It was in this
calling by name that Mary recognised the risen Christ.
She responded in an intimate form of address, 'Rabbuni'
or my 'My dear Rabbi'. Now that she had found him she
longed to cling to him, something Jesus would not allow.
This was not because he wished to keep her at a distance,
it was John's way of telling us that the form of intimate
communion which we shall have with Jesus comes
because he has ascended to the Father and has sent the
Holy Spirit. It is through this Holy Spirit that we come
into a life-giving relationship with the risen Christ, the
conqueror of death. Jesus had to tell Mary, and through
her the Christian community, that he was with them in
a way that does not rely on the need for the physical
body, even his resurrected one. It is his Spirit living
within them and within us that gives new life and new
freedom.

What then does this story of the grief of Mary and her
meeting with Jesus have to say about finding freedom in
times of bereavement?
Mary grieves – we grieve. First the story tells us that
Mary searched for the body of Jesus. She had seen him
die. She knew the reality of death and she longed to do
what she could for his body. Death is real. We are right
to do what we can for the mortal remains of those we
have loved and we have the right, too, to grieve over our
loss. Just as Mary stands weeping in the garden because
she cannot find Jesus, we too may stand and weep
because we have lost someone we love who was known
to us and present to us in a physical body. Wanting to do
what we can as a last act of love for this person is natural
and right.

Mary doubts – we doubt. Second we notice that in
John people often see on the surface but never understand

the reality that lies beneath. We have many stories in
the Gospel where people see but fail to believe. The disciples see the risen Lord and yet do not recognise who it
is. We can see death and we see on the surface the horror
of a life ended, of an apparent extinction of existence. It
all seems so final. For some a belief that life goes on is
very difficult. That there is an existence beyond what we
see is very difficult to grasp. Jesus appears to Mary and
she doesn't recognise him. This can give us hope for those
times when we doubt that there is a life after death. We
are in good company when, like Mary, we fail to recognise that things are different from what we see.

Mary needs time – we need time. Third it takes time
for Mary to recognise Jesus. So too, it may take time for
us to recognise that death is not the end. Our life will
never be the same again without our loved one but the
story tells us it is possible to find a new phase of living.
Just as it takes time for Mary and the other disciples to
come to terms with the new way that Christ is with
them, so it takes time for us to come to terms with the
departure of our loved one and the new way in which
our life must now be lived. Jesus is with them in a new
way, a new form of existence. Similarly our loved ones
are in a new form of existence but they are none the less
real.

Mary is called by name – we are called by name.
Fourthly, the story tells us that each of us is loved and
known by name. God called each of us by our name. That
intimate communion of being called personally as unique
individuals will not cease with death. To God we are not
a flock of sheep all looking the same, we are known
intimately by name. So we can have confidence that our
loved one will continue to be called by his or her name.
That uniqueness will not cease to be on their physical
death.

Mary discovers Jesus anew – we discover Jesus anew.
Finally Mary longs to cling to Jesus, her risen Lord. She

has to learn that he is now with her in a new way. We long to cling to our loved ones. The story tells us that like Mary, we have to learn that they are with Christ in a new way. What can give us the greatest freedom of all is to know that they are in Christ and Christ is in us. His spirit lives within us. He is with us in a new way and so are they. Mary had to learn to let go of the Jesus who had walked with her and had died on the Cross. She had to find him in a new way and she could only do that when she let go of the past and stepped into the future.

FOR REFLECTION

1. Place yourself and all who are dear to you alive or dead in the presence of God.
2. Ask yourself how times of bereavement have affected you. How has your faith altered because of it? How has your image of God changed? What positive and negative things have you discovered?
3. Read the passage from John 20 again.
4. Try to imagine the scene under the different emotions Mary goes through.

PRAYER

Close with a time of prayer in your own words or using the following psalm.

> Yahweh is my shepherd, I lack nothing.
> In grassy meadows he lets me lie.
>
> By tranquil streams he leads me
>   to restore my spirit.
> He guides me in the paths of saving justice
>   as befits his name.

Even were I to walk in a ravine as dark as death
I should fear no danger, for you are at my side.
Your staff and your crook are there to sooth me.

You prepare a table for me
    under the eyes of my enemies;
you anoint my head with oil;
    my cup brims over.

Kindness and faithful love pursue me
    every day of my life.
I make my home in the house of Yahweh
    for all time to come.

(Psalm 23)

Freedom from Fear of Death

TONY WAS WALKING around the cemetery. It was a warm and pleasant day with the breeze gently swaying the trees. He read the gravestones as he passed. 'Mary Evans, Beloved Wife of Albert, Died 18th May 1884, Aged 73.' Tony walked on. 'Philip Martin. Aged 4, Died November 12th, 1964. May he rest in peace.' Tony shuddered and suddenly felt cold. It would come to him sometime. One day he would be like Mary Evans or little Philip returning to dust; the body he now cared for decaying away. He turned and walked quickly out of the cemetery. Even away from the cemetery it scared him. The thought that one day he would no longer exist as he existed now. He hated to think about it. Not only his own death but the death of others, of those he loved.

Tony was a practising Christian but, if he was honest, there were times when he wondered if there really was anything after death. He couldn't bear to think that he would cease to exist and yet he sometimes wondered if the Christian insistence that life goes on wasn't just a way of trying to cope with the horror of the finality of death. Somehow death seemed so frightening, so indescribably 'other'. Tony knew he could not run away from his fear of it forever. But he had no idea how to cope with it.

In the Gospel according to St John we have the story of one family's experience of coming face to face with death. It is the story of Mary, Martha, and their brother Lazarus and of what happened when Jesus arrived at the family home just after Lazarus had died and been buried.

Mary went to Jesus, and as soon as she saw him she threw herself at his feet, saying, 'Lord, if you had been here, my brother would not have died.' At the sight of her tears, and those of the Jews who had come with her, Jesus was greatly distressed, and with a profound sigh he said, 'Where have you put him?' They said 'Lord, come and see.' Jesus wept; and the Jews said, 'See how much he loved him!' But there were some who remarked 'He opened the eyes of the blind man. Could he not have prevented this man's death?' Sighing again Jesus reached the tomb: it was a tomb with a stone to close the opening. Jesus said 'Take the stone away.' Martha, the dead man's sister, said to him, 'Lord, by now he will smell; this is the fourth day since he died.' Jesus replied, 'Have I not told you that if you believe, you will see the glory of God?' So they took the stone away . . . he cried in a loud voice, 'Lazarus come out!' The dead man came out, his feet and hands bound with strips of material and a cloth over his face. Jesus said to them, 'Unbind him, let him go free.'

(John 11:32–41, 43–44)

In St John's Gospel the story of the raising of Lazarus is a crucial one. The first part of the Gospel contains a series of 'signs' by which Jesus shows who he is and what he has come to give to humankind. These signs provoke both faith and opposition in those who witness them. The raising of Lazarus is the high point of these signs. In it John tells us a number of things about Jesus and what he has come to do.

The story of the death and raising of Lazarus prefigures the death and raising of Jesus. Just as Lazarus has died and come to life again, so too Jesus will die and rise from the dead. Lazarus stands for all Christians. Just as Jesus raised him so he will raise us all from the dead. Furthermore it is through Jesus that death is overcome. When Jesus dies life is conferred to all who believe. The story tells us what Jesus' death will do. Jesus dies but rises again. He will give life to us, as to Lazarus. So death and the horror of it is conquered in Jesus.

For John death is seen on different levels. There is physical death, but there is also spiritual death and the two are not separated in the same way as we think of them as separated. For the author, not to believe is a sort of death. To believe in Jesus is to have life, to reject Jesus deliberately is to walk the way of death. So, although this story is about physical resurrection it is also about Jesus giving life in the spiritual sense, what John calls elsewhere 'life in all its fullness'. John's account of the public ministry of Jesus often has hidden meanings within it. Death in the story is spiritual as well as physical. Here then there is a struggle going on between physical death in life and also between spiritual death in life. Unbelief and rejection leads to death. Faith in Jesus leads to life. The battle has raged throughout the Gospel and it reaches its highpoint here in this story.

Another important element in the story concerns the reality of physical death. John wants us to be quite sure that Lazarus is dead. We hear that he has been in the tomb for four days. We read that Jesus has no doubts about the death of this friend of his. He weeps. That weeping was not so much for the death of a friend, after all, Jesus is about to raise him, but it is a weeping for the darkness and sadness which death itself brings. In the face of the bleakness and reality of death and the distress it causes Jesus is moved. He is 'deeply moved in spirit'. That phrase also contains an element of anger in it. Perhaps when face to face with the horror of death, Jesus experiences anger that it can cause so much pain to humankind. Clearly Jesus faces the reality of death when he comes to Bethany, just as he will have to face the reality of his own death in Gethsemane. That we should be 'deeply moved in spirit' by death, should not surprise us.

When Jesus actually raises Lazarus, John recalls the miracle itself in a very few short sentences. Jesus performs for Lazarus what he promises to do for each of us. He calls out with a loud voice for Lazarus to come from the tomb; the loud voice being the sign of power. When Lazarus appears Jesus' command is to 'Unbind him, and let him go free'. Lazarus is to be loosed from the shackles of death and freed to walk in the newness of life. Jesus' power means that death has lost its sting. It is conquered.

John has many points he wishes to make in the story of the raising of Lazarus. We noted that the raising of Lazarus prefigures the death and raising of Jesus. It is because Jesus died himself that we can know two things. The first is that he has faced it himself and so understands the horror of it. The second is that through his death, life triumphs, so, although death may still hold its terror for us, and we may still fear it, death is not the conqueror. Jesus is the victor.

Facing fear. The next thing to note is the insistence John has that death is very real and we cannot escape facing it. Bodies decay and moulder. Death is not pleasant. Jesus is in great distress in the face of the darkness of death just as we often are. We feel cheated by it; by its apparent finality which is so unfair. Yet one of the ways we can begin to be free of our fear of death is to understand the fear and face it as Jesus did. To do so is to begin to rob it of some of the power it can hold over us.

Trusting the risen Christ now. Another necessary

attitude is to begin to see, with John, that death comes in many forms of which physical death is one. John's desire that the Christian community should understand that Jesus comes to give life *now* and that life is abundantly rich can help us in our struggle to overcome our fear of the physical death. If we can begin to live the life of the risen Christ in the here and now and discover his presence with us now then physical death does begin to lose its sting. A risen Christ whom we trust and know and who is present with us will not desert us at the moment of death. If we know him now, why should we fear that he would leave us at the moment our bodies die. Spiritual life is for the present and leads to life in all its fullness now and in the future. Rejection of that gift offered is death as we are missing out on what God wishes us to have.

Unbound and free. Finally the story reminds us that what Jesus wants is our freedom. He wants to 'unbind us and let us go free' just as he wanted that for Lazarus. That freedom is from death in all its forms. It is a freedom which comes to us as a free gift and it is a freedom Christ gives because he has gone before us, facing all that we face. It is because of who he is and what he has done that his freedom is now ours. Death in all its forms has no more dominion over us. He has set us free.

FOR REFLECTION

1. Spend a moment of quiet in order to recollect yourself.
2. Ask yourself what frightens you about death. Why? What doubts do you have, if any, about life after death?
3. Use the following saying of Jesus. Say it over and over again as a mantra. Allow yourself to hear Jesus saying these words to you.

        I am the Resurrection and the Life

Allow his life to flow into you. Do this for as long as
you wish.
4. Pray for those who are dying that they may be aware
of the presence of Christ, the risen Lord.

PRAYER

You might like to close with the following prayer or one
of your own.

And now, thus says Yahweh.
he who created you, Jacob,
who formed you, Israel:
Do not be afraid, for I have redeemed you;
I have called you by your name, you are mine.
Should you pass through the waters, I shall be with you;
or through rivers, they will not swallow you up.
Should you walk through fire,
    you will not suffer,
and the flame will not burn you.
For I am Yahweh, your God,
the Holy One of Israel, your Saviour.

(Isaiah 43:1–3)